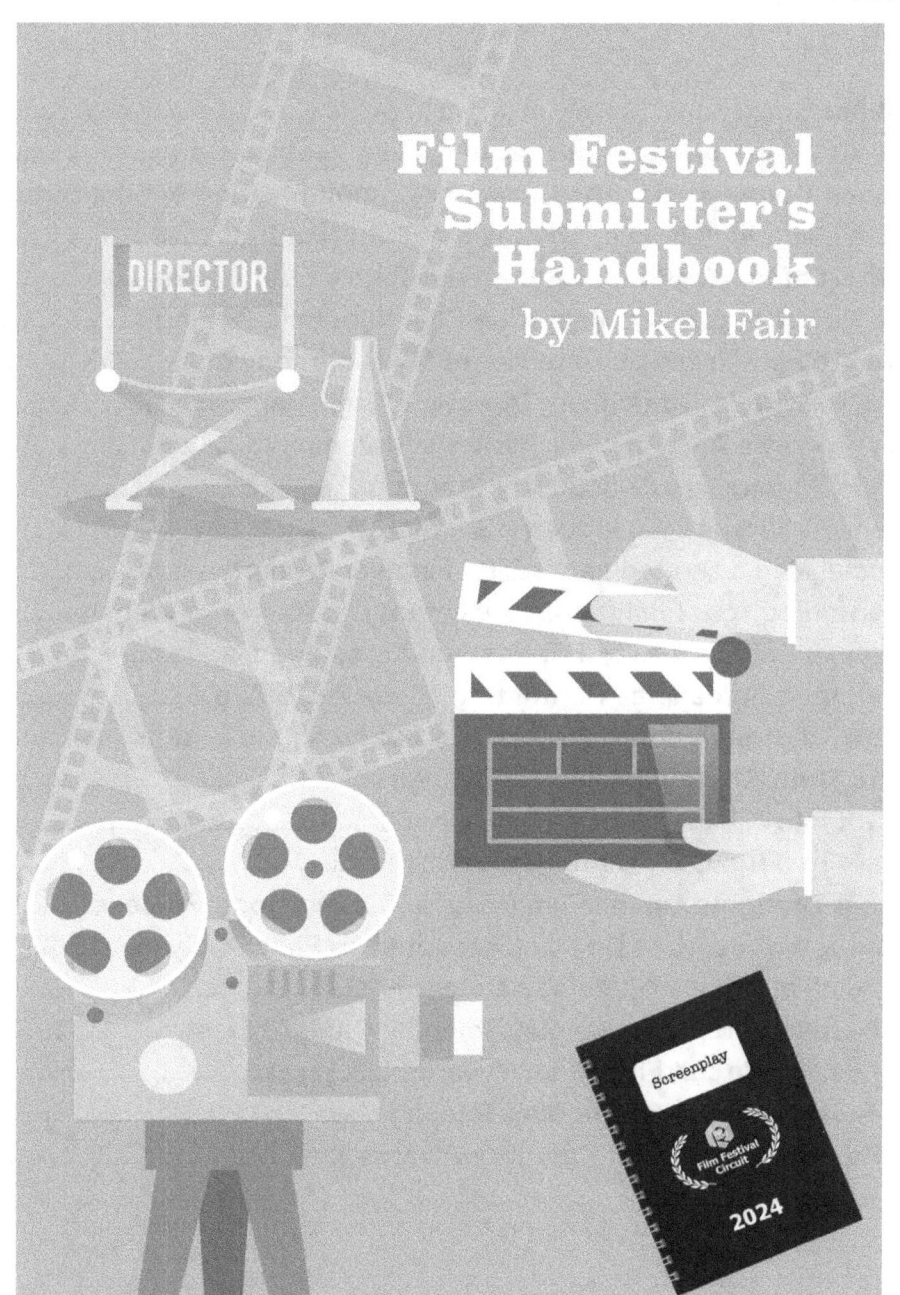

Film Festival Submitter's Handbook
by Mikel Fair

Table Of Contents

Chapter 1: The Art of the Submission: Crafting Film Festival Gold

Have you ever received multiple gifts for a birthday, holiday, or another special occasion? Consider how you chose which gift to open first. Was it the biggest, the shiniest, or the heaviest? Did you shake or smell them? The packaging often sets expectations about its contents. Imagine receiving a small, wrinkled, damp paper bag with no markings – would you anticipate finding something valuable inside? Conversely, what if you were given a large, smooth, shiny box adorned with a pretty bow and a thoughtful card? Wouldn't that excite you? Packaging matters. It doesn't alter what's inside, but the perception that a better wrapped gift contains something superior is common. Perhaps that unappealing, damp paper bag hides a valuable diamond, while the attractive box only holds a worthless rock. Barring practical jokes, such extremes are unlikely on your special days. Drawing from over a decade of experience in film festivals and having evaluated over 6000 film and screenplay submissions, I've observed a significant trend. Too many filmmakers are submitting their work to film festivals with inadequate packaging.

My name is Mikel Fair, and I have been involved in the film industry since the 1990s. In 2008, my wife Brooke and I began accepting submissions for the Houston Comedy Film Festival, marking our first foray into event organization. This venture was inspired by my own experiences as a filmmaker who submitted work to various film festivals. Now, we manage 12 different events across Texas, Oregon, and Georgia. Over the past 15 years, we have gained substantial knowledge, and the industry has evolved significantly. As of 2024, the film festival circuit is more competitive than ever. Despite this, filmmakers and screenwriters continue to repeat many of the same errors. This insight comes from my personal journey in the industry.

In 2006, I produced a short comedy film and submitted it to 10 film festivals. The rejections began to arrive, causing me distress. Each submission cost me between $35 and $75, and I was only accepted into one event. Receiving those dreaded rejection letters was disheartening, and I started to doubt myself. My aspiration of presenting my film at a festival, winning awards, and standing on stage in front of a large audience began to seem unattainable. I believed that winning festival awards could pave my way to joining the Directors Guild of America (DGA) and directing a major studio film. However, reality set in, and I was plagued with self doubt and despair. At that time, I didn't realize my submission had several drawbacks. I was making costly errors without any awareness of them. I had invested my heart into creating this 26 minute comedy, which I thought of as a "masterpiece," yet it was almost universally rejected. I couldn't understand why it was being turned down. The film was humorous, the sound quality was good, we used high end equipment, and I had an experienced crew and talented actors. My friends even laughed at the film's content. The rejection letters left me confused and upset.

I began to point fingers, making statements like, "these film festivals are political," or "they probably stopped watching after the first minute," and "my movie doesn't have enough stars, so it was likely overlooked." I also noticed that none of the festivals provided feedback. I wondered if anyone had actually watched the entire film. Could it be that an intern watched a few minutes and then discarded my DVD? Despite cashing my submission fee, I received nothing in return. I blamed everyone except myself until a friend suggested I focus more on my film's presentation. He was referring to the poster and DVD cover. Back in 2006, submissions were physical, requiring a mailed DVD, unlike today's digital submissions. Another friend mentioned the film's long duration and extensive, slow credits as potential issues. When asked if I had a trailer, I was dismissive, questioning its necessity for a short film. I assumed festivals would simply play my film for a good laugh. I was wrong. My marketing was virtually nonexistent – a white labeled DVD in a jewel case with the film's name and tracking number handwritten in permanent marker. I hoped a festival judge would discover it among thousands of submissions and immediately recognize its brilliance. But this was unrealistic, especially considering many festivals I submitted to selected only 25-30 films. I was rapidly losing money and not thinking clearly about the process. I realized there was a gap in my understanding of the Film Festival Circuit. Faced with this reality check, I had to decide: should I invest more time and money to improve this rejected film, start a new project and discard the old one, or cut my losses?

I painfully realized that, months after completing the film, I was the only one still deeply invested in it. The cast and crew had moved on, partly because the project wasn't finding success and also because I wasn't providing any updates. When we got accepted into our first film festival, I texted a few friends, naively expecting word of mouth to spread the news globally. I made a Facebook post about the festival acceptance, which received a few likes, but at the festival screening, aside from my wife, only two crew members attended, both of whom had already seen the film several times. I lacked marketing expertise and was unsure how to effectively promote the film.

Realizing the need for a change, I decided to stop placing blame, set aside my ego, and reassess my approach. Two months later, after improving the presentation and reediting my film, I resubmitted it to 10 more film festivals. Astonishingly, it was accepted into 9 of these events. This success was both unexpected and incredibly gratifying.

As a child, whenever my father advised, "Mikel, learn from others' mistakes," I'd dismissively reply, "Duh, whatever, Dad." It seemed like such a cliché, something you'd find in a fortune cookie. But as I grew older, I realized the profound truth in his words, especially in business where mistakes can be costly in both time and money. Learning from others can spare you immense grief and frustration.

This book is designed to save filmmakers and screenwriters time and money. I meticulously detail practical strategies for crafting a strong submission to film festivals. More importantly, I share my personal journey of transforming an initially unsuccessful short film into one that gained widespread acceptance in the festival circuit. While I can't guarantee a magic formula to get your film accepted into every festival, this book is written to help you enhance your submission package. First impressions are crucial. Demonstrate to festival judges the care and thought you've put into your submission. Stand out among the myriad of films and screenplays you're competing against. Consider this book your secret arsenal. I wish I had such a guide when I started; it compiles years of experience, and I'm still learning every day. If you have questions or topics you'd like me to address in future editions, feel free to email me at mikel.fair@filmfestivalcircuit.com. Best of luck, and happy reading!

Chapter 2: Missed Connections: The Impact of Communication in Film Submission

Here's a true story. At one of our earliest film festivals in Oregon, we chose a local Portland film featuring a cast and crew from the area. Most of them lived within a 10 mile radius of our venue. The director was nominated for the "Best Director Award," and the lead actor for the "Best Actor Award." The director was our main point of contact, and we communicated by email for three weeks leading up to the event. He expressed great excitement about the screening. I offered him a choice between a Friday or Saturday night slot during the two day event, and he eagerly chose the opening slot on Friday night. This was the first short film screening of the evening, expected to draw a large audience. I was surprised when he arrived at the screening with just his wife. Inquiring about his cast and crew, he nonchalantly responded, "I don't know if they are coming." I found his comment strange but had to attend to other duties.

The screening went splendidly, with lots of applause and even some whistles during the credits. I assumed his cast and crew had shown up after all. But, just five minutes after his film ended, the director and his wife abruptly left the theater, even though there was over an hour and a half left in the program. Catching up to them, I asked if everything was alright. He mentioned having 'dinner plans' set months in advance. This, too, seemed odd to me, but we parted ways after a handshake.

The following day, Saturday, was our awards ceremony. His film had two nominations. When I announced it as the winner of the "Best Actor Award," the audience applauded, but no one came forward to accept the award. With no representatives from the film present, I was clearly perplexed. I set the award aside, mentioning to the audience that I had seen the director the previous night and expressed hope that he was alright. After the festival concluded on Saturday night, I texted him to check in, but received no response.

On Sunday, a friend invited me to visit the set of his film, which was being shot at a brewery in downtown Portland. Having not been on a film set for some time, and after a busy festival weekend, I welcomed the opportunity for a break. Returning to a film set felt refreshingly familiar: the bustling crew, dolly tracks, actors getting makeup done, and the general buzz of production. While observing, I noticed a few actors rehearsing their lines in a corner. To my surprise, there was the lead actor who had won the Best Actor award just the day before. I couldn't help but wonder why he hadn't shown up to receive his award or why I didn't recall seeing him at the screening on Friday night.

Hours later, after his scene wrapped up, the actor was saying his goodbyes and preparing to leave. I approached him as he headed to his car. "Hey," I said, "you're the actor from the film we screened on Friday at the film festival I organized. Excellent performance, it's great to meet you." He gave me an awkward handshake, looking at me as if I were an overzealous fan. He responded, "Yeah, thanks man, I remember that film. Where did you see it?" I mentioned the festival's name and the fact that he had been nominated for an award weeks earlier. He was completely unaware of this. We walked outside together. I opened my car trunk and retrieved his award. Handing it to him, I saw him become emotional. "Dude, I won? I've never won anything before! I work in construction and barely have time for acting. My wife and daughter keep pushing me to act. They've been eager to see this film, but I've had no updates." His passion and genuine excitement were evident. There we were, standing in a parking lot, just miles from where the award ceremony had taken place the day before. I shook his hand, feeling sympathy for him missing his big moment. He also hadn't heard from the director and was quite disappointed.

The director, who was our main contact, never provided an explanation for his absence. To this day, I'm in the dark. He failed to inform his crew about the screening, didn't share any of our social media posts about his film on Facebook or Twitter, and his production company's website didn't mention the festival or the film. He didn't communicate through text, email, or any updates, and didn't invite the 25-30 local people involved in the film to the festival. He also never responded to my text message from Saturday night. A few days after the event, he unsubscribed from all communications using the email address I had for him. Since then, I've neither seen nor heard from that director again.

This brings to light the importance of your role when you submit to a film festival and are listed as the only contact. You wouldn't believe how many filmmakers are difficult to reach, disorganized, or too overwhelmed to manage festival related matters. While it's understandable given our busy lives, work commitments, and personal responsibilities, it's crucial to stay engaged. If you're too busy to manage festival communications, ensure that someone reliable and available from your team is assigned as the point of contact. I've seen filmmakers and screenwriters spend over $1000 on submission fees only to vanish. Years later, their films might appear on YouTube with minimal views, and they barely mention any festival acceptances. My first film was like my baby; I treasured every email, framed my award certificates, displayed the event badges, and talked about its achievements everywhere, perhaps to an annoying extent. However, it's disheartening to see that some people, whether due to indifference or busyness, fail to manage their film's festival journey properly.

Effective communication is crucial in the relationship between film festival submitters and event teams. It's surprising how many submissions we receive that lack a valid phone number or email address. Each year, we have to reject films simply because the email provided bounces, leaving us no way to download their video file for the screening.

When a phone number is available, I typically send a text to notify the submitter of the email issue. Given the intense competition in the film festival circuit, such an oversight can be costly. Discussing this with other festival directors, I've realized my approach isn't universal. Some directors told me, "You texted them? I don't bother. I just mark them as 'not accepted' and move on." It's unfortunate to reject submissions for such a reason. To avoid this, I suggest the following when filling out your film festival submission form:

1. Use an email address you frequently check and ensure its spelling is correct.
2. Include your phone number in the submission details. Film festivals are not commonly known to sell phone data to marketers.
3. About 30% of submitters don't provide a phone number, possibly due to privacy concerns. However, submitting to a film festival is different from signing up for an unknown app. A call from a festival is typically positive news.
4. In your cover letter, mention the email addresses and phone numbers of a couple of alternative contacts from your crew.
5. By 2024, some find it easier to be reached via social media platforms like Instagram, Twitter X, or Snapchat, rather than through traditional phone numbers, which might be ignored if unknown or from out of state. If this applies to you, include a social media handle you frequently use.

I always make a habit of responding to every email I receive, treating my inbox like a to-do list. I reply to each email as thoroughly as possible and then archive it to keep my inbox and mind organized. If I'm unable to address an email immediately, I mark it with a star and leave it in my inbox until I can deal with it. This approach is also beneficial for film festival submitters. It's common to receive a flood of requests and updates from multiple film festivals, which can lead to confusion over events and dates. We often notice communication issues with disorganized submitters at every festival. Frequently, we receive questions that have already been answered in the initial acceptance email or on the event's public webpage:

- "I didn't realize I was accepted until a friend mentioned it on Facebook."
- "I was unaware of my award nomination."
- "I've forgotten the venue address. Where is it?"
- "How do I obtain tickets?"
- "I just discovered we're screening at your event. What should I do?"
- "I just found all your emails in my spam folder!"

Creating separate folders for each film festival that accepts your film can be helpful. This way, you can quickly access vital information without extensive searching. Promptly responding to film festival emails is crucial—it shows that you're engaged, active, and easily reachable. Also, remember to express gratitude upon receiving an acceptance email. Film festival organizers often work for little to no compensation, many as volunteers. Treat interactions with them differently than you would with a large corporation's call center; these organizers are likely filmmakers, screenwriters or film enthusiasts like you. Surprisingly, many people accepted into our festivals fail to say "Thank you."

A note on email service providers: Responding to emails signals to your provider (like Gmail, Hotmail, Apple, etc.) that communication with that sender is important. If you ignore several emails from a film festival, don't be surprised if future communications end up in your spam folder. Make an effort to reply to the festival, engage in the conversation, and keep the communication lines open.

Chapter 3: From Generic to Iconic: The Craft of Film Naming

In recent years, we've received over twenty five submissions titled "Swipe Right." While those filmmakers might have thought the title was fitting or inventive, few realized that many other films might share the same name. A distinctive title can help audiences recall your film; think about how "Return of the Jedi" or "The Walking Dead" are more memorable than generic names like "Space Film" or "Zombie Show." Choosing a unique and less common title is wise for several reasons. Firstly, film festival attendees often want to recall their favorite films. Secondly, similar titles in a competition can confuse festival judges. Lastly, search ability matters; if someone wants to research your film online, will they easily find it?

I've noticed that attendees at film festivals I've hosted often struggle to remember specific films. Questions like, "What was the film about two girls and their mom on a road trip?" or "Which one had the tall guy, the short guy with the baseball cap and mustache, and the odd girl with the small dog?" are common. These queries usually result in ponderous looks and finger snapping as people try to recall. A title that encapsulates a key aspect of your film can aid memory.

For instance, at the Austin Comedy Film Festival one year, we screened "The Milkman" and "Milk Man" — two entirely different films with different plots, actors, and countries of origin. One was a romantic comedy about a woman's affair with a milkman, while the other was a dark comedy about a milkman discovering a dead body. More descriptive titles like "Guess What The Milkman Found In The Bushes?" or "The Milkman That Wouldn't Shut Up" or "My Baby's Daddy Is The Milkman" would have been more memorable. These might be humorous examples, but they illustrate an important point: a title that includes a specific detail can make your film or screenplay more memorable to festival attendees.

Consider the challenge of distinguishing your film with commonly used titles like these, especially when searching online:

- Addiction
- Anonymous
- Besties
- Blind Date
- Carpe Diem
- Choices
- Cut
- Dirty Work
- Dreamer
- The Wingman
- Right Swipe
- Swipe Left

Consider this: film festival judges handle hundreds of films and screenplays during their judging process. You want your submission to stand out in their memory. Judges might sift through 500 submissions over 10 months. Picture a room with 12 judges, each with a tablet, surrounded by coffee, pizza, and stacks of paper notes, on the day before notification day. It's frustrating when they ask, "Which one was 'Blind Date' again? Was it the one with the blonde girl and the dark haired guy, or was that 'The Blind Date'?" A dash of creativity in naming can make a significant difference. Titles like "Blind Date with Angie," "Not Another Blind Date In Miami," or "My Blind Date Couldn't See Me, Literally" might have been more distinctive. A good comedy title often elicits laughter just by itself. Remember, it's not just attendees and judges trying to match titles with films; search engines can get confused too.

In today's world, where quick online searches dominate and people often don't look past the third or fourth result, a memorable title is crucial. People frequently use their phones or type full phrases into social media and search engines. For example, when someone asked me the name of our comedy film festival in Portland and couldn't find it online, it turned out they were searching for "Oregon Movie Festival" instead of "The Portland Comedy Film Festival." Such misunderstandings highlight the importance of an easily searchable and memorable title. Titles like "Forrest Gump" or "Ferris Bueller's Day Off" stick in people's minds, but not every title does. Search for "Carpe Diem" on IMDb, and you'll find over 100 results; "Blind Date" brings up over 200. A unique or specific title helps people remember and find your film or screenplay more easily, whether they're festival attendees, judges, media, or distributors.

On our website, we list the full film name, the directors' names, and the country of origin for each selection when announcing our official selections. Thus, a search for "sisters kill misters portland comedy film festival" yields relevant links, including our website. Think about what comes up when you search for your submission. Making your film or screenplay easy to find and remember with a unique title is key to standing out in the crowded film festival landscape.

Chapter 4: The Art of the Tagline: Crafting Your Film's First Impression

Crafting a compelling tagline for your film is a skill in itself. It should succinctly and memorably encapsulate the essence of your film. Here are ten tips to help you create an effective tagline:

1. Summarize the Theme: Ensure your tagline concisely reflects your film's central theme or message.
2. Stir Curiosity: Your tagline should intrigue the audience and make them eager to learn more.
3. Emotional Connection: Engage your audience's emotions, whether through humor, suspense, romance, or mystery.
4. Brevity is Key: Aim for a short, impactful tagline, ideally under ten words.
5. Uniqueness: Avoid clichés and tailor a tagline that's distinctive to your film.
6. Match the Film's Tone: Your tagline should align with your film's genre, whether it's comedy, drama, horror, or other.
7. Clever Wordplay: Use puns, alliteration, or other linguistic techniques for a catchy tagline.
8. No Spoilers: Intrigue without revealing crucial plot points.
9. Imagery Through Words: Use your tagline to create a vivid mental picture.
10. Feedback Loop: Experiment with different taglines and seek opinions to find the most effective one.

Understanding the difference between a tagline and a synopsis is crucial for film festival submissions. A tagline is a catchy, brief phrase used for marketing, meant to attract and intrigue an audience without revealing too much. In contrast, a synopsis is a straightforward summary of the film or screenplay's plot, and is typically 100 words or less. Every festival, I see submitters film in the tagline and synopsis with the exact same sentence. Initially, I mistook them for being similar, which led me to avoid writing either. This was a mistake I soon realized. This chapter will focus on guidelines for writing effective taglines, while the next chapter will delve into synopses.

As a Film Festival Director overseeing selection teams, our primary goal is to promote the selected films and screenplays. As a filmmaker, it's vital to craft your own marketing language to control the narrative about your work. Leaving the "Tagline" and "Synopsis" fields blank in your submission form is a missed opportunity. It risks having someone else possibly misrepresent your film if accepted.

Taglines should be catchy and memorable. For instance, "The Matrix" (1999) uses "Welcome to the Real World," a phrase that hints at the film's alternate reality theme. "Ferris Bueller's Day Off" cleverly uses "One man's struggle to take it easy," and "Alien" is known for "In space, no one can hear you scream."

It's a common error for submitters to begin their synopsis with what is essentially a tagline. For instance, instead of starting with a lengthy sentence like "When two men find their mother dead, they search for clues throughout the house," a more effective approach is to use a concise, intriguing hook such as "Two brothers investigate their mother's murder, but the clues point to each other." A tagline should spark interest and mystery, and it needs to be clearly distinguished from the synopsis. If you're too immersed in your project to see this difference, consider getting feedback from friends, former teachers, or crew members. Experiment with various options and see which ones have the strongest impact. The following chapter will delve into the significance of crafting a compelling synopsis for film festival submissions.

Regarding film festival submission portals, you might have noticed that many don't offer a specific field for a tagline. Although I've suggested this feature, it's yet to be implemented. In the meantime, you can use the available synopsis field. Start by typing 'Tagline:', followed by your tagline, then 'Synopsis:', and proceed with your synopsis. This workaround ensures that festivals, particularly those that value this information, can easily distinguish between your tagline and synopsis. We hope to see this feature added soon for more streamlined submissions.

Chapter 5: The Power of Brevity: Mastering Film Synopsis Writing

A synopsis is a public description that provides the audience with a sense of your film's genre and plot. Often, filmmakers find it challenging to write a synopsis, worrying about revealing too much. If writing isn't your strong suit, seek help. Have someone watch your film or read your screenplay to craft a concise synopsis. Aim to keep it under 100 words. Some filmmakers and screenwriters err by writing synopses that are around 1000 words, resembling detailed breakdowns rather than succinct summaries. Avoid this approach; it's impractical to effectively convey a story in less than 10 minutes using 1000 words. Of course, the length of your synopsis will vary based on your film's duration. For a 60 second film, the synopsis will naturally be shorter. For a feature film or screenplay, it might be slightly longer than 100 words, but excessive length is not advisable. Exercise good judgment and try to stay within the 100 word limit whenever possible.

Here are examples of two different synopses with optimal length, leaving just enough mystery and not revealing the end of the story.

> *"Peter's Birthday Gift" is a romantic comedy film that follows Peter Larkin, a seventeen year old high school student. Peter is interested in two different girls and can't decide which one he'd like to date. He decides to base his decision on the gift each girl gives him for his birthday. Which gift will Peter choose? Seeking advice, he turns to a friend who secretly plans to give Peter a gift he never expected.* **(74 words)**

> *"Last Resort" is an action packed drama film about a woman named Charlene, who is preparing to rob a poker game in a dangerous neighborhood. When she asks her best friend and ex-con, Alice, for help, it puts both of them in a precarious situation that will change their lives forever.* **(50 words)**

A compelling synopsis is essential; it should summarize the plot without spoiling the ending, enticing viewers to fully engage with the film or screenplay. Equally important, yet often overlooked, is specifying the genre. This becomes particularly noticeable in "all genre" film festivals, where attendees frequently seek specific genres. A synopsis that clearly states the genre can attract an audience specifically interested in that type of film. This is vital for screenwriters too. In my experience hosting film festival awards ceremonies, winners often express interest in particular genres, such as relationship dramas or comedies. A clear genre designation in your synopsis can help connect your work with those actively seeking that specific genre. Neglecting to specify the genre can lead to frustration among potential viewers, especially if the synopsis is too vague to identify the film's nature, be it horror or comedy.

Here's an intriguing statistic: at the Texas Short Film Festival in the summer of 2023, about 15% of the 200 submissions received had no synopsis at all – that's roughly 30 submissions with no description whatsoever! This oversight forces festival staff to interpret and describe these films, a risky approach when you've invested significantly in festival submissions. To avoid having your story inaccurately represented from memory, it's crucial to provide a comprehensive synopsis.

Moreover, when preparing to market official selections, a considerable amount of time is spent communicating with submitters to gather missing elements like taglines, synopses, directors' statements, writers' statements, posters, images, and trailers. This back and forth process not only consumes valuable time needed for social media promotion and creating marketing materials but also highlights the importance of the relationship between submitters (screenwriters and filmmakers) and the film festival. Having a ready-to-go synopsis enhances this relationship and aligns the goals of both parties in marketing the event. A well prepared synopsis helps to generate excitement among potential festival attendees, encouraging them to attend your film's screening or inquire about your screenplay.

Chapter 6: Why Do Film Festivals Care About My Biography?

Do you ever find it challenging to talk about yourself? The inevitable question "So... what do you do?" seems to come up in every new encounter. Often, it feels like an indirect inquiry into how you earn a living, which can be stressful. However, in the context of film festival submissions or networking events, the focus shifts more towards your role in the film and television industry. Preparing in advance for this question can significantly streamline the conversation. Adhering to a few simple guidelines can help you respond to this frequently asked question effortlessly and confidently.

The "Writer's Biography" or "Director's Biography" section on your film festival submission form is often neglected or left blank by screenwriters and filmmakers. Many might feel that their filmmaking experience isn't extensive enough to mention, or believe it's irrelevant. Some may underestimate the importance of their background in other industries. Often, directors and writers are hesitant to self promote, preferring to let their work speak for itself. While this approach is admirable, I believe omitting the biography when submitting to film festivals is a missed opportunity.

A common pitfall for film festival applicants is the submission of excessive information in their biographies. Detailing every single day at a university, theater group, film set, or television show can be excessive and counterproductive, overshadowing the intended brief summary of "who you are." Film festivals value your biography as it provides judges and potential viewers with a glimpse into the creators' background and their role in the project. For instance, knowing that a writer of a government conspiracy thriller previously worked at the NSA for a decade, or that the director of a romantic comedy about a businessperson falling for a bartender once co-owned a bar in a college town, adds depth and context to their work. When crafting your biography for film festival submissions, focus on experiences that have influenced your creative content. This differs from a synopsis, writer's statement, or director's statement. Your biography can remain relatively consistent across submissions, especially if they share a thematic or topical connection, while synopses, writer's statements, and director's statements should be tailored uniquely to each screenplay or film. Further details on writer's and director's statements will be discussed in the following chapter.

Attendees at our film festival events frequently ask, "Who made these movies?" For many potential viewers, the concept of a film festival is entirely new. A concise biography, limited to less than 150 words, can help attendees understand the creator's origins and their career stage. This information often helps viewers connect with the creators. For example, someone might say, "Oh, this screenwriter grew up in Queens, just like I did," or "This documentary should be interesting; the bio mentions the filmmaker worked at the EPA for 20 years." A well crafted biography also gives insights into the future aspirations or potential next steps of the director or writer. It's crucial to differentiate between a director's or writer's biography and a resume. You're not applying for a job; rather, you're sharing the life experiences that have shaped your journey as a director or screenwriter, which is what genuinely intrigues people. Consider these definitions:

> Resume (or Résumé): [rez-oo-mey]
> > A brief written account of one's personal, educational, and professional qualifications and experience, prepared typically by an applicant for a job.

> Biography: [bahy-o-gruhf-ee]
> > A written account of another person's life.

A director's or writer's biography blends elements from both a resume and a traditional biography. It can be thought of as "a brief written account of personal, inspirational, and professional experiences that shaped an individual's journey to becoming a director or writer."

From the submissions we receive daily at our festivals, it's evident that many filmmakers approach their bios as if applying for a job. We often see biographies exceeding 1000 words, detailing every aspect from high school plays to fast food customer service roles. While it's acceptable to mention such experiences if they are relevant, brief, and have significantly influenced your filmmaking aspirations, the key is moderation. People are naturally curious about who you are, and it's fine to share your achievements, educational background, and previous work that led to your current submission. However, moderation is crucial — a 1000 word biography can be overwhelming. A more concise, impactful bio is far more effective and engaging. Trust me on this.

When preparing your director's or writer's biography, it's beneficial to contemplate and answer the following questions to create a compelling and relevant profile:

1. Where did you grow up? - This gives context to your cultural and geographical influences.
2. Where do you live now, or where are you based? - This information can reflect your current cultural and professional environment.
3. How long have you been a director or writer? - This indicates your level of experience and dedication to your craft.
4. Are there any work related experiences that influence your filmmaking or screenwriting today? - Mention if you have a background in fields like marine biology, law, skating, caregiving, academia, yoga, customer service, etc., especially if they impact your filmmaking style or content.
5. What are some creative works that inspired you to become a director or writer? - Cite specific TV shows, films, or novels (like 'Jaws,' 'Maid In Manhattan,' 'Orange Is The New Black') that sparked your passion.
6. Who are some creative individuals who inspired you to become a director or writer? - Acknowledge influential figures in the industry, such as Spike Lee, Amanda Tapping, Stephen King, Susan Collins, etc.
7. What's next? What is currently in development? - Share a glimpse of your future projects or plans, providing a sense of direction and ambition in your career.

By addressing these questions thoughtfully, you can craft a biography that's engaging, informative, and reflective of your unique journey and aspirations in the world of film and writing. These biographies provide a solid foundation, but they can be refined for clarity and impact:

Jennifer Sanders' Fictional Biography

> *Jennifer Sanders, originally from Tennessee, now resides in New York, where she is a freelance Art Director. Inspired by observing experienced directors on set, Jennifer embarked on directing two short films in the past two years. Her first, a comedy, echoes the style of 1980s Dan Aykroyd and Chevy Chase classics. The second, a drama, draws inspiration from the popular TV show "This Is Us." Both shorts are currently being showcased in various film festivals. Sanders is also in the process of developing a Romantic Comedy series pilot, a project inspired by her experiences and relationships back in Tennessee.* **(99 words)**

Director Silvia Coy's Fictional Biography

> *Silvia Coy, grew up near Detroit, Michigan, ventured to Southern California at 18 to pursue her passion for filmmaking. After graduating from film school, she returned to Michigan to direct her first short film, 'Lasting Memories,' marking her directorial debut. Her experience in college, working on several short film crews, laid the groundwork for her directorial journey. Silvia plans to move back to Southern California to work as a 2nd Assistant Director on the studio feature film, "Saving Chloe." Her ultimate ambition is to direct a feature film for a major production company, a goal she is steadily working towards.* **(100 words)**

This next fictional biography gets a little wordy and runs a bit too long. Sometimes half of the biographies we receive are written like this.

> *John McCartheson is a director, writer, best boy grip and editor that currently lives in Santa Fe, New Mexico, but grew up in Albuquerque. John has several film credits, some of which are on IMDb and others are uncredited. Award winning films like the Vegetable Detective, Gone Boy, Bizarre Food Truck Adventures as well as two days on the new Transformers spinoff "Bumblebee" film where he worked as a production assistant on the 4th unit. John has been named to the Dean's list 3 times in his academic career. Once at the University of Southern New Mexico and twice at Shale Film School where he is set to graduate later this year. John has scored an A or a B in every film related class. His first student film, McCartheson directed the comedy film, Living With Billy Black, three years ago. Billy Black finished 3rd in the audience choice award voting at the San Juan International Film Festival, was an official selection to the Norwich Mountain Goat Film Festival and Screenplay Competition. It was also an official selection to the San Antonio Giggle Fest, but the film did not screen because the projector wasn't working. Billy Black was nominated for Best Editing at the Northwest Short Film Festival but a local film won the award, because the editor was a judge for the festival, but whatever. John starred in seven high school plays including McBeth, Romeo and Juliet, The Wonderkin, Free For All and a play that his friend Rachel Marks wrote called Straight From Southshore. These experiences propelled his career in filmmaking to new levels. After meeting Adam Sandler's stunt double at a previous film festival, John has been preparing a screenplay that will be handed directly to Adam Sandler when it's finished. Hopefully he will get an opportunity to direct a film with his hero.* **(308 Words)**

Indeed, receiving detailed Director's Biographies like the ones provided is common, and it's certainly preferable to receiving no information. However, it's important to remember that overly lengthy bios may be subject to editing by film festival staff to fit the program's format and style. Relying on festival volunteers to edit your biography might result in changes that don't fully align with your preferred presentation of your career and accomplishments.

To avoid this, it's advisable to have a few trusted individuals review your biography before submission. Their feedback can help ensure that the bio is concise, clear, and accurately represents your journey and current projects. Striving for brevity without sacrificing the essence of your story is key. A well edited and succinct bio not only fits better in festival formats but also makes for a more enjoyable read for the audience, enhancing their connection with you and your work. Here is a revision of the example above.

> *John McCartheson, a Santa Fe based filmmaker, balances his roles as a grip and production assistant in New Mexico's independent film scene with being a rideshare driver, a job that often inspires his film characters. A part time student at Shale Film School, he anticipates graduating this year. In 2016, McCartheson directed "Living With Billy Black," a micro comedy film that garnered selections from seven film festivals and a Best Editing nomination at the Northwest Short Film Festival. With a passion for filmmaking ignited by high school theater classes, his ultimate goal is to direct a comedy starring Adam Sandler. Currently focusing on expanding his directorial portfolio, John seeks a comedy screenwriter to collaborate on developing new short film concepts and ideas.* **(120 Words)**

Understanding how to craft a director or writer's biography is crucial in creating a connection with your audience. Highlighting the career stage of the director or writer is particularly important, as it sets viewers' expectations during screenings and fosters a sense of familiarity. Attendees often express admiration for productions, especially when they learn of a filmmaker's novice status, like being a first time director.

Moreover, people are usually intrigued by a filmmaker's future ambitions. Independent films often serve as pivotal career milestones for emerging directors and screenwriters, acting as practical resume items. These projects are not just creative expressions but also stepping stones for future opportunities. The goal is for viewers to leave a film or screenplay reading not just entertained but also curious about what you'll do next. Ideally, they should be motivated to follow you on social media, engage with your content online ("liking" or sharing your trailer on YouTube), or bookmark your website for future updates.

In addition to the biography, there's another aspect that you should consider including in your submission form. It might not be part of your biography but could fit well in your writer's or director's statement. I'll discuss this further in the next section.

The importance of highlighting local and regional connections in film festival submissions cannot be overstated, especially since many festivals, like ours, have a keen interest in these aspects. It's perplexing that around 25% of submitters overlook including this information, potentially due to a misconception or misguided advice. This omission can have significant consequences, as illustrated by an incident at the Austin Comedy Film Festival.

In this instance, we had a category for the "Best Texas Film Award," but only three Texas based films were nominated because it appeared that no more qualified. However, after reaching out to filmmakers for location details, one particular film stood out during the festival for its audience appeal and buzz. Unfortunately, the filmmakers weren't present and had been unresponsive to earlier communication. Upon contacting them post-event, we learned that their film was actually shot in Texas, but this information was not indicated anywhere on their submission form. They had assumed they weren't nominated for the "Best Texas Film Award" due to perceived lower quality of other films. This was a revelation, as their film would have been a strong contender for the award had we known its Texas origins.

This story underscores the value of clear communication and the importance of providing comprehensive information in film festival submissions. A well filled submission form, including bios, director's statements, and specific details like shooting location, can significantly influence the success of your submission. Such details are not just administrative; they are integral to how your film or screenplay is perceived and categorized in the festival circuit.

Chapter 7: How To Write A Compelling Director's Statement

This is probably the most overlooked and forgotten box on the film festival submission form. Don't miss this opportunity to explain your personal motivation, inspiration, experiences and challenges that lead to the creation of your submission. Unlike a biography, which talks about the general background of the content creator, the director's statement is more personal as it pertains to the specific submission that the judge or festival attendee is about to experience. Try to limit your Director's Statement to 150 words or less.

At most of our festivals, only about 50% of submission forms include a Director's Statement at all. Some people aren't sure what to write for this box so they seem to put anything in here. Recently someone wrote "I love Horror Films, Blood and Guts. I hope you like it." Another person stated, "If Charlie Chaplin and Charles Manson had a baby, you would truly understand what you just saw." To this day, I still don't know what that means. I encourage you to take this seriously. What inspired you? Was this an opportunity to use a specific location, actor or equipment? Is there a personal experience related to this film? Unlike a Director's Biography, the Director's Statement explains your personal connection to this particular story.

Here is a list of statements in no particular order that may be helpful when writing your director's statement. Try filling in the blanks. This should give you a nice start.

1. I chose to direct this film because …
2. While watching this film, I wanted the viewer to experience …
3. Some of the challenges making this film included …
4. I was inspired by the work of (blank) to create this film …
5. Working with these actors was special because …
6. Working with this crew was fun because …
7. We were fortunate to get the equipment for this film because …
8. We were fortunate to get the location for this film because …
9. This film will always be special to me because …
10. The film turned out to be a little different than the script because …
11. We had some delays creating this film because …
12. We were fortunate to raise the funds for this film by …
13. The experience working on this film will help me with future projects because …
14. I decided to make this particular film because …
15. This idea came about because …
16. The way I went about my casting call was …
17. Producing this film took about "X" number of days because …

Here are two fictional Director's Statements that offer personal insight into the creation of each film.

I directed "Teen Broken Promises" inspired by personal experiences. A friend, Sheila, moved far away and later spread rumors about me, leading me to realize she wasn't a true friend. The film's protagonist, Elsa, echoes this experience. Initially planning to confront her friend Julia over past lies, Elsa discovers Julia's struggle with depression and suicidal thoughts. My volunteer work at a women's shelter, where I encountered many women battling dark thoughts, shaped Elsa's journey. Her initial anger transforms into sympathy, choosing support and love over confrontation. This film was a cathartic process, helping me heal from past wounds, even as Sheila's fate remains unknown. **(104 words)**

Here is another fictional Director's Statement example that is shorter, but effective.

Our casting journey led us to Connie, whom we discovered through a comprehensive search. Her exceptional table read captivated us, and her performance in the film is both powerful and emotionally resonant. Remarkably, a Craigslist ad brought her to our audition, leading us serendipitously to the ideal fit for the role. This experience demonstrates that great casting decisions often extend beyond familiar networks. Sometimes, reaching out through a casting call to those you don't know can uncover a hidden gem. **(80 words)**

This third version of a fictional director's statement is effective, because it answers most of the common questions that I hear asked at film festival Q&A sessions.

When my co-writer, John Robles, and I began writing "John The Angry Mover," we were inspired by his experiences and anecdotes from moving furniture in Houston, Texas, during the 70s and 80s. John's encounters provided a wealth of material for a fantastic comedy. Having met several actors and comedians on previous sets, we also organized casting calls for them. We managed to shoot the film over three full days, braving the intense Texas summer heat, but the experience was incredibly enjoyable. **(81 words)**

This Director's Statement provides a clear insight into the film's creation and its personal significance. Crafting such a statement is not just a formality; it's a preparatory step for future interactions, such as Q&A's at film festivals. From personal experience, writing a Director's Statement has been instrumental in framing my film's pre-production context. It's common to see directors struggle with basic questions during Q&As, often leading to uncomfortable moments. By investing time in a well thought out Director's Statement and practicing responses to common questions, you can avoid such awkwardness and engage more confidently with your audience. Trust me, you'll be grateful for the effort you put in now.

Chapter 8: How To Write A Compelling Writer's Statement

Similar to the principles of writing a good director's statement, in that personal motivation is important, for screenwriters, a crucial aspect to highlight is the significance of the writer's statement in a slightly different way. Despite the assumption that screenwriters, being writers, would easily provide such a statement, this is often not the case. For instance, at our Houston Comedy Film Festival Winter 2024 event, almost half the entrants omitted this key piece of information. When contacted, many were willing to provide it, yet it seems they may not fully grasp its importance. This statement reveals the writer's personal drive behind their screenplay, a factor we emphasize at our film festivals, particularly during award presentations. The audience, in rapt attention, seeks to understand not just the story but its origin. Try to limit your Writer's Statement to 150 words or less.

Remember, when presenting a screenplay, it typically hasn't been produced yet, so the audience relies on this insight to visualize and connect with the story. Screenwriters often draw from personal experiences – be it a tragedy, a humorous incident, a family matter, a frightening experience, or even a dream. This is your chance to share the motivations, inspirations, and challenges that led to your screenplay's creation, whether it's part of a movie trilogy, adapted from a book, a long-held story idea, or inspired by specific actors, settings or experiences.

Unlike a biography that provides a general background, the writer's statement delves personally into your specific submission, enhancing its appeal to judges, investors, producers, and agents seeking particular genres or ideas. Your personal narrative can pique the interest of the right individuals in a way no one else can.

See if you can answer as many of these questions as possible when you write your writer's statement.

1. Why did you choose to write this particular story in this genre?
2. What made you decide to write this as a feature film, short film, or teleplay/series episode?
3. Do you plan to create a sequel or continuation for this story?
4. What creative works inspired or influenced this story?
5. Were there any specific writers or directors who inspired this story?
6. What inspired the personalities and traits of the characters?
7. Have you visualized any actors who could potentially play the roles?
8. What personal experiences, if any, influenced the plot and situations in the story?
9. Do you plan to produce this film/episode yourself, or are you seeking a production company to acquire the rights?
10. Do you intend to release this story in other formats like a book, audiobook, or novella?

Here is a fictional example of a writer's statement for a feature length screenplay:

> *I chose to write "Space Renegades," a feature-length screenplay, for its definitive ending, allowing viewers to ponder the characters' ultimate sacrifice to save the world. This story, without plans for a sequel, is a tribute to my passion for space military combat films, particularly those like "Aliens," "Starship Troopers," and "The Expanse." Directors Ridley Scott and Neil Blomkamp have been significant influences. In envisioning the cast, I see Vin Diesel as the ideal Judd and a younger Emilia Clarke as Mindy. The film, rooted in my childhood fascination with future technology and weaponry, is rich in these elements. My goal is to sell the screenplay to a major studio, such as Fox or the SyFy Channel. Depending on future opportunities, I might also adapt "Space Renegades" into a book and audiobook.* **(131 words)**

If you decide, as a screenwriter, to attend a film festival, your goal should be to meet people and do some networking. When you have a good writer's statement and can easily talk about what your screenplay is about and your motivations for writing it, your conversations will be a lot smoother.

Screenwriter participation at film festivals is often lower than that of filmmakers. Reasons vary, from shyness to uncertainty about attendance unless assured of an award. However, it's essential to recognize that the value of film festivals extends beyond winning. These events are about sharing your story, connecting with an audience, and embracing the community, not just the accolades.

Chapter 9: Movie Posters Are An Industry Standard

Movie posters have been a cornerstone in film industry marketing for decades, serving as the initial visual representation of a film, video, or screenplay. These posters often feature a compelling image or a collection of images that encapsulate key elements of the submission, along with credits for notable members of the production team such as the lead actors, director, composer, and cinematographer. It's common to see studio and production company logos included as well. The enduring appeal of movie posters is evident, with some people collecting them for their historical and artistic value.

However, despite their proven effectiveness in marketing, many independent filmmakers overlook this traditional step when submitting to film festivals. This could be due to concerns about the costs associated with creating a poster. Yet, the impact of a well designed poster should not be underestimated. Think about your own experiences at a movie theater, arriving early and browsing the posters on the walls. A captivating poster can pique your interest, leading you to consider watching the film with your family, or discovering an awaited sequel. This initial intrigue often prompts further exploration, such as watching the trailer online or reading early reviews to decide if the movie is worth your time and money.

This process mirrors the decision making journey of film festival attendees. As they choose which sessions to attend, a striking and thoughtfully designed poster can significantly influence their selections. Thus, investing in a quality movie poster can be a crucial step in attracting attention and generating interest in your film at festivals.

Your movie poster plays a pivotal role, enabling film festivals to effectively market your film. When filmmakers omit a poster from their submission form, it complicates our marketing team's efforts significantly. To address this, I often find myself sending out emails, a time consuming task that ideally shouldn't be necessary, to multiple filmmakers who have been selected for our festivals. An example of such an email is as follows:

"Hello, I am Mikel Fair, the director of the Film Festival Circuit. Congratulations on your selection for one of our festivals. I noticed your film's submission form lacks images, which are essential for our social media promotion. Could you please provide these at your earliest convenience? Thank you. We eagerly anticipate marketing and showcasing your film at our upcoming event."

Despite this outreach, responses vary; some submitters update their submissions promptly, while others do not. The reason for the inconsistency in responses to this seemingly straightforward request remains unclear to me.

Here are five compelling reasons to create a poster for your film festival submission:

1. First Impression: The official poster often forms the initial impression for most viewers of your film.
2. Generating Interest: Information on your movie poster can spark intrigue in your festival screening session.
3. Marketing Tool: Film festivals frequently use film posters for social media promotions and articles.
4. Photo Opportunities: At film festivals, movie posters serve as excellent backdrops for photographs.
5. Memorable Keepsake: Printed movie posters become a cherished part of your film's history.

Aim to design a poster that captures attention and represents your submission effectively. Standard dimensions for movie posters are 11w×17h inches or 18w×24h inches, with 11x17 being the most common size we receive. When our film festivals announce official selections, we showcase every poster on social media and use the most striking ones to decorate the event venue. These posters not only enhance the festival atmosphere but also spark curiosity and conversation.

However, in 2023, 25% of submissions we received lacked any image on their festival submission form — no poster, headshot, screenshot, or behind the scenes photo. Additionally, 35% of submissions had images, but they were either not in a poster format or lacked text. Remember, a poster without your name or essential information hardly connects with your submission.

A compelling movie poster includes the film's title, an engaging visual element, and names of the director, writer, stars, and production company logo. Update it with Film Festival Laurels as your film garners accolades. While "A Picture Is Worth A Thousand Words" holds true, the text on your poster is equally significant, offering a potential hook with the release date, tagline, and credits.

If you're unsure how to add an image to your Film Festival Submission Form, here's a link to a 60 second tutorial: https://youtu.be/3ftHVe3jls

For DIY poster creation, try the Canva Poster Maker. It's user friendly and allows for quick image generation and export. Check out this tutorial, which includes a guide on adding Film Festival Laurels to your poster: https://youtu.be/waT1Ev_6Nd4

This process is straightforward, even for those without Photoshop experience. Don't miss this simple yet effective marketing opportunity.

Chapter 10: Film Trailers Are An Industry Standard

As a Film Festival Director with over a decade of experience, I highly recommend creating a trailer for your film or series before submitting to film festivals. While not a prerequisite for acceptance, trailers are invaluable to our judging and marketing processes.

Our judges watch every video submitted, including trailers, which aid in recalling details of your film, especially weeks after the initial viewing. This is crucial during both the selection and award nomination phases, as judges frequently reference, rewatch, compare, and spot check submissions before finalizing their ratings.

For accepted submissions, festival attendees often decide which sessions to attend based on their knowledge of the films. Trailers provide a sneak peek of what to expect, incorporating video, dialogue, music, and sound effects. We promote every accepted film's trailer on event pages, ticket pages, and social media, enhancing excitement about your work.

Trailers also serve as a gateway to your film's website or social media, answering attendees' queries about release notifications and sharing options. Including a link in the description of your trailer expands its utility, directing viewers to more information about your other productions.

Film festival submission portals allow uploading of trailer video files or public links (Vimeo or YouTube). This facilitates our use of your film's video clips (without sound) for commercials or advertisements. For sharing purposes, a public Vimeo or YouTube link is preferred to avoid issues with inappropriate content or copyrighted music. Plus, it keeps control of the trailer's availability in your hands.

Online engagements with your trailer (Likes, Shares and Comments) serves as free marketing and a public record of interest. This can be crucial if a distributor researches your film; seeing a trailer with significant views and engagement are always beneficial.

In our Oregon Short Film Festival Summer 2023 event, just over half of the submissions had trailers. A good trailer can strengthen your submission and give you a competitive edge. Consider if you'd buy a ticket to a film festival without trailers; most attendees, like consumers, prefer to know what they're watching before committing time and money. Sessions with engaging trailers tend to have better attendance. In a world where trailers often influence moviegoing decisions, your film's trailer can be a decisive factor in attracting an audience.

For maximizing the effectiveness of your film trailer on Vimeo, consider these strategies:

- No Viewing or Sharing Restrictions: Ensure your trailer is accessible to all by removing any view or sharing restrictions. This facilitates sharing on social media and embedding on other websites, thus broadening your film's reach.

- Enable Downloads: Allow users to download your trailer. Film festivals might use parts of it, sometimes without sound, in their promotional materials, which aids in marketing your film as part of the event.

- HighQuality Resolution: Upload your trailer in the highest resolution possible. While 720p was once a standard, UHD (3840x2160) is now widely supported and offers superior quality on streaming platforms. A high resolution trailer is less likely to appear compressed or pixelated when included in high quality festival montages.

For YouTube, keep these points in mind:

- Remove Restrictions: Ensure your trailer is fully accessible by removing any view or sharing limitations. Avoid using 'unlisted' videos as they can restrict the trailer's visibility.

- Optimize The Thumbnail Image: Select a thumbnail that is both visually appealing and representative of your film. An engaging thumbnail can significantly increase the likelihood of someone clicking on your video.

- Encourage Initial Engagement: Boost your trailer's visibility by asking your crew, family, and friends to watch, rate, comment and share it. Since YouTube's view counts are public, high initial engagement can create a positive impression.

- Be cautious with Music: Try to avoid copyrighted music. YouTube offers a free music library that won't risk a copyright strike. Alternatively, if you have a composer, ensure it's a work for hire agreement, giving you full rights. If your composer distributes the music elsewhere, your trailer would later be flagged for copyright, jeopardizing accumulated views, comments, likes, and shares.

- Adhering to these guidelines on Vimeo and YouTube can significantly improve the impact of your film trailer, ensuring it reaches and engages a wider audience effectively.

When crafting an effective film trailer, consider these four essential tips:

- Incorporate Essential Text in the Video: Always include the film's title, director, and main stars within the video file itself. Relying solely on the text title and description outside the video is insufficient. Remember, your trailer might be shown in various contexts where external text isn't visible. Including this information directly in the video ensures viewers always know the name of your film.

- Include a Call to Action (CTA): At the end of your trailer, display a CTA for 45 seconds, like a website or social media link. This is crucial because festival attendees frequently use their phones to look up more information, share the film, or contact the creators. A CTA in your trailer capitalizes on this opportunity for engagement.

- Don't Hesitate to Reveal Your Story: The fear of "giving away the story" often hinders filmmakers. However, it's important to show enough content to intrigue and motivate viewers. A trailer doesn't need to reveal everything but should provide enough incentive to watch the full film. A few images and music excerpts can be effective without spoiling the story.

- Create a 'Clean' Public Version of Your Trailer: Ensure there's a version of your trailer suitable for all audiences. This is particularly important for films with explicit content, like profanity laden comedies or graphic horror films. Social media platforms, YouTube, and Vimeo may restrict or ban trailers with offensive content, negatively impacting your marketing efforts. It's fine to have a mature version, but don't rely on it for broad marketing purposes.

Adhering to these tips can significantly enhance the effectiveness of your film trailer, making it an impactful tool for marketing and promoting your film or series episode at festivals.

Chapter 11: Social Media Strategies for Film Festival Promotion

Social media has become an integral part of society, weaving its way into the fabric of our daily lives. In its early days, around 2009, when we began using Facebook to promote film related posts, there was considerable resistance. Many established screenwriters and filmmakers feared the exposure of their ideas and preferred to keep their projects under wraps. Today, while some still harbor these concerns, the majority of filmmakers and screenwriters embrace the visibility that social media provides. Announcements of film festival acceptances and achievements on platforms like Facebook, Instagram, or Twitter become exciting news to share with a broader audience. These platforms serve as powerful, cost free marketing tools for promoting Film Festival submissions.

I recommend including a business Facebook Page, an Instagram profile, or a Twitter X account on your film festival submission forms. You might wonder why this is necessary, especially if you're not a fan of social media or believe it lacks industry relevance. However, it's important to recognize that these platforms have evolved beyond their initial uses. What was once perceived as a space for personal anecdotes, like sharing a meal on Twitter X, has transformed into a dynamic platform for film industry professionals to share updates and engage with audiences about their work. Social media provides a cohesive way to keep the cast and crew connected postproduction and to broadcast updates to a wide audience. Today's reliance on social media often surpasses that of traditional email, making it an indispensable tool for filmmakers.

Contrary to some outdated views, social media is not just about casual updates. It's a forum for generating genuine interest in your creative content, attracting likes, comments, and engagement from a global audience. It's about establishing a presence in a space where the film industry, fans, and potential collaborators can easily find and interact with your work. Therefore, incorporating social media into your film festival strategy is not just advisable; it's essential in the modern digital landscape.

There are two effective strategies for leveraging social media to promote your film or screenplay. The first involves creating a dedicated account for each specific project. This is particularly useful if your work is brief, like a short film or screenplay. The alternative is to establish a single profile across different platforms for all your creative endeavors, whether it's for writing, directing, or your production company.

Starting with the first approach, you can create a social media page specifically for your film or screenplay. For example, a page titled "Last Train To Everwood Documentary Film" or @LastTrainToEverWood. Your posts can be straightforward, focusing on updates and milestones related to your project. Ideal content includes:

1. Announcements of acceptances or official selections at film festivals.
2. Notifications about award nominations.
3. Updates on newly received laurels.
4. Sharing positive feedback from judges.
5. Unveiling new posters featuring your latest laurels.
6. Announcing your attendance at film festivals.
7. Posting photos and stories from festival events.
8. Wearing custom merch or clothing showing your support for film festivals.
9. Creating engaging reels and videos from your festival experiences.
10. Sharing experiences and connections made at film festivals, including live updates.

Platforms like Facebook enable you to create events for film screenings or festival appearances. It's beneficial to collaborate with festival organizers on these posts for cross promotion. Instagram also offers features for collaborative posting, enhancing the reach and engagement of your content.

For those who prefer a broader approach, setting up a social media account for your production company, screenwriting, or directorial work is effective. This can be something like @rosewildproductions, @writer.jenna.shields, or @director.mel.smith.

It's important to recognize the power of social media in making your work visible and searchable online. If a film festival mentions your submission, engaging with their post shows your involvement and appreciation for the recognition. Similarly, interacting with posts about other projects can build mutual interest and expand your network, a critical component in promoting your involvement in film festivals.

To manage your social media presence efficiently, focus on your preferred platform and direct followers there from other accounts. Regularly schedule posts to maintain a consistent online presence without it overwhelming your schedule. You can delegate this task to someone on your team, ensuring a steady stream of content even during busy periods.

In today's digital age, having a visible online presence for your work is crucial. A lack of online buzz can significantly hinder your project's marketability. Adapting to these changes and utilizing social media effectively can greatly enhance your project's success and visibility in the film industry.

Chapter 12: Centralize Your Film Industry Content On Your Own Website

The significance of a film website in today's digital landscape was the subject of a recent discussion I had with a filmmaker from the Middle East. Despite his impressive resume, spanning 15 years and 35 films with various awards and nominations, he surprisingly revealed that in his country, creating websites for films is considered a waste of resources. Instead, he relied on scattered online presences, such as tweets and a partially accurate IMDb profile, leading to a disjointed digital footprint.

Contrastingly, I believe a website is crucial for any film submission. It serves as a centralized hub, offering comprehensive information and a controlled narrative of your work. For instance, our Film Festival Circuit website is a continually evolving platform, hosting a wealth of information including event listings, blog articles, a direct submission portal, submission rankings, scorecards, and past event highlights, all linked to our social media.

A basic film website should encompass essential elements like a tagline, synopsis, bio, director's statement, and relevant images such as posters and headshots. It should also feature a list of festival selections, nominations, awards with links, your trailer, social media accounts, links to other creative projects, and a contact form. This setup ensures your website answers critical questions about your involvement in film projects, the genres you work in, access to non-public material, distribution status, festival accomplishments, affiliations, and any related press.

Here are the key elements of a film website organized as bullet points:

1. Tagline: A short, memorable phrase that captures the essence of your film.
2. Synopsis: A brief overview of your film's story and characters.
3. Bio: Background information on you as the filmmaker/screenwriter.
4. Director's Statement: Your vision and approach for the film.
5. Images: Film poster, headshots, production photos, etc.
6. Festival/Award List: All official selections, nominations, laurels, with links.
7. Trailer Link: Embed or link to your film trailer.
8. Social Media: Links to relevant accounts like Facebook, Twitter, etc.
9. Other Projects: Links to your previous or upcoming creative work.
10. Contact Form: Allow viewers to directly email you.

Your website should answer 10 key questions:

1. How to contact you?
2. Number/types of projects you've created?
3. Where to view a list of your produced projects?
4. The genres represented in your work?
5. How to request access to unreleased material?
6. If your projects have distribution?
7. Your films' festival accomplishments?
8. Key talent or organizations attached?
9. Published articles about you or your work?
10. Where can I follow you on social media?

The goal is for your website to provide a comprehensive snapshot of your film's history, achievements, social media engagement, and contact points. An optimized, well organized website can rank highly in search results over time. It should also be featured on your business cards and marketing materials for better visibility. The filmmaker I mentioned took the hint and created a website for his production company, showcasing each film he worked on through blog posts. This central hub significantly increased his company's work engagements and inquiries about his festival achievements.

I have some advice for screenwriters as well. As far as screenplays, whether or not to make them public on your website really depends on what you are trying to accomplish. If you're a screenwriter, you should have a website or social media profile that makes it easy for agents, distributors, and producers to see all of your festival awards in one place. If you've registered your screenplay with the US Copyright Office (or its equivalent in your country), I don't see any harm in posting your work publicly. However, to track your leads, I recommend providing a contact form or email address where someone can request your screenplay and provide some information about themselves. Are they a distributor, agent, or producer? Where did they hear about your screenplay? Collect an email address, phone number, and business name if possible. All of this information can be very useful, and you can even send them periodic updates as you get selected for more film festivals and earn accolades.

Creating a website today is simpler than ever, with tools like WordPress, GoDaddy, and Google Blogger that require no coding skills. While some filmmakers may not see the immediate value in having a dedicated website, its benefits in terms of SEO and credibility are undeniable. A website is a more stable and permanent showcase of your work compared to the volatile nature of social media platforms. It's also important to consider cost effective hosting solutions and remember that website expenses are tax deductible business costs. A well constructed website is indispensable for a filmmaker or screenwriter. It not only serves as a comprehensive archive of your work but also enhances your professional image, ensuring that anyone searching for you online finds a cohesive, up-to-date, and impressive portfolio.

Chapter 13: Crucial Editing Advice For Festival Screenings

For Film Festival programmers, efficient use of time is crucial. This is especially true in events like the Austin Micro Film Festival Spring 2023, where a vast array of short films are showcased in limited time blocks. With only a fraction of the audience typically connected to each film, it's vital for filmmakers to consider the impact of their film's length and content in terms of festival programming and audience engagement.

I advocate for creating two versions of your film: the "Final Cut" and the "Festival Cut." The Final Cut is your unabridged version, including every credit and detail, ideal for online platforms and private screenings where every contribution can be celebrated. On the other hand, the Festival Cut is streamlined, focusing on maintaining the festival's pace and audience attention. It should introduce the film quickly, within 15-30 seconds, and keep end credits to a minute or less. This version should still acknowledge key cast and crew members and include a clear call to action, like a website or social media link at the end.

While film length doesn't exclusively determine festival selection, overly long credits or intros can negatively impact your film's reception. A concise Festival Cut not only respects the festival's schedule but also improves the chances of your film standing out in a competitive environment.

In re-evaluating my own film, I conducted a personal experiment. I screened my 26-minute comedy to different groups of friends, observing their reactions rather than the film itself. This approach revealed what genuinely resonated with the audience and what didn't. I asked specific questions to garner constructive feedback, focusing on characters, plot elements, dialogue clarity, and potentially offensive content. This feedback was instrumental in transforming my film into a more concise, 13-minute version, cutting out parts that didn't add to the story or were technically flawed.

I learned the importance of ensuring every element, including b-roll, directly contributes to the narrative. Dialogue should quickly establish the film's purpose, and both the introduction and credits should be succinct. Based on audience feedback, I also adjusted the film's language, reducing profanity to make it more accessible, and added a content warning for mature language.

My experience highlights the importance of being receptive to feedback and willing to make tough edits for the sake of your film's success on the festival circuit. A well-edited Festival Cut can significantly enhance your film's appeal, making it more likely to be selected and well-received at film festivals.

When preparing your film for festival submissions, it's essential to make every second count while respecting the contributions of everyone involved. Here are some key points to consider for a successful submission:

1. Streamline Your Introduction. Keep your film's intro, including production company logos, concise - ideally under 30 seconds. This helps captivate your audience right from the start, immersing them in your story without delay.
2. Craft a Compelling Opening Scene: The first scene of your film should be exceptionally well-written and engaging. It's your first and best opportunity to hook your viewers and set the tone for what's to come.
3. Optimize B-Roll Usage: Long B-roll shots can disrupt the pace of your film. Aim for brief and impactful B-roll and transition scenes, around 2-3 seconds, to maintain momentum and keep your audience engaged.
4. Concise End Credits: Avoid lengthy, scrolling black credits. Keeping your end credits under 60 seconds can significantly improve the pacing of your film and hold the audience's attention until the very end.
5. Reconsider Outtakes and Inside Jokes: While outtakes and inside jokes can be fun, they often don't resonate with an audience unfamiliar with the context. Consider whether they add value to your film for a broader audience.
6. Effective Call-to-Action: Provide a clear call-to-action, such as a website, social media handle, or QR code. This encourages interested viewers to learn more about your film, explore extended versions, or connect with your work on other platforms.
7. Streamlined Credits for Festival Cuts: In the festival version of your film, it's not necessary to give each credit a separate black card. This approach isn't about disrespecting your crew but about adapting to the film festival environment. Shorter credits are particularly important if your team isn't present at the screening.

Remember, these guidelines are about making your film more appealing and accessible to festival audiences and judges. Every decision you make should enhance your story and showcase your team's hard work in the best possible light.

Chapter 14: Common Screenplay Formatting Mistakes To Avoid

Screenwriters often make critical mistakes in formatting and submitting their screenplays to film festivals. Our technical scorecard deducts points for common errors such as:

1. Missing Title Page Credits: Many screenplays lack "written by" or "story by" credits on the title page. Never assume the festival knows who wrote the screenplay. Always include proper credits. For instance, in our Fall 2023 festival, 30% of submissions lost points for this oversight.

2. Lack of Contact Information: It's vital to include at least one contact detail (email, phone number, or website) on the title page. This prevents your work from getting lost or mixed up if printed for review. Surprisingly, half of the screenplays at the same festival failed to include contact information, a critical step often overlooked.

3. Submission Format: Many entries are incorrectly submitted in Microsoft DOCX or Final Draft FTX formats. Since judges may review submissions on various devices, and not all have the necessary software, it's crucial to submit in PDF format. This ensures compatibility across all devices.

4. Correct Category and Page Count: Ensure your screenplay matches the page count for the intended category: Shorts and Teleplays under 60 pages, and Feature Length over 60 pages. Misplaced submissions in incorrect categories can lead to grading errors and submission fee discrepancies. Additionally, judges are compensated based on page counts, and errors in categorization can cause billing issues.

5. Industry Standard Structure and Format: Surprisingly, 5% of submissions resemble short stories or essays rather than screenplays. Screenplays should adhere to industry-standard formatting, which includes specific details like time of day, scene descriptions, characters, wardrobe, locations, and props. Using professional screenwriting software can help maintain these standards.

Avoiding these common errors can significantly increase your screenplay's chances of success at film festivals.

Chapter 15: How To Stretch Your Film Festival Submissions Budget

Years ago, when I completed my first short film as mentioned in the introduction of this book, I was taken aback by the unexpected financial demands of the process. Beyond the submission fees, which are just the tip of the iceberg, there were expenses like event tickets, travel, accommodation, and meals, not to mention taking time off work. As a freelance production sound mixer, my income depended on my availability for last-minute jobs, adding to the financial strain. Juggling these costs with life's responsibilities, such as childcare and special occasions, was a daunting task, and I know this struggle is common among many in the film industry.

Despite some high-end festivals covering travel expenses, the reality is that most film festivals, especially without consistent substantial sponsorship, can't afford to do this. So, what can you do when your film or screenplay is being celebrated at festivals and you're not sure how to reduce the cost of attendance?

Here are some tips that I've found helpful:

Budget for Festival Submissions and Attendance: Before you start filming, include marketing and festival expenses in your film's pre-production budget. Often, filmmakers focus heavily on equipment costs, overlooking post-production marketing expenses like submission fees and travel.

Submit Locally or Where You Have Connections: Save on accommodation by staying with friends in the festival city where you're submitting. It's often cheaper than hotels and rental cars, even if you buy your friends tickets to attend.

Opt for Driveable Festivals: Festivals within driving distance eliminate the need for air travel and allow more flexibility in your schedule. Packing food for the road can also save on meal costs at restaurants.

Consider a Side Hustle for Extra Income: I turned to driving for Uber to fund my festival submissions. This flexible job allowed me to earn extra money in my free time, specifically dedicated to covering festival costs. It's about setting small, achievable financial goals to support your festival journey. You can earn at least $1410 for your first 130 passenger trips in 30 days. Here's our affiliate Uber link for those interested in a similar path where you can earn: https://drivers.uber.com/i/kp5r6qs577vt

Look for Submission Discounts: Always check for promo codes and discounts when submitting to festivals. For instance, we offer a 20% discount code for our festivals, and many filmmakers miss out on these savings. Here are two useful links for festival submission discounts:

https://filmfestivalcircuit.com/blog/filmfreeway-promo-codes and
https://filmfestivalcircuit.com/submissions

Ask Festivals About Discounts: If you can't find promo codes, don't hesitate to contact festival organizers to inquire about possible discounts. While it's more challenging to get full fee waivers, asking for discounts often yields positive results.

Crowdfunding works! Small campaigns for $500-$750 can be very successful on https://seedandspark.com/ If you're trying to raise under $1000 and you take the time to go into great detail about what you're spending the money on and why, you have a better chance of meeting your goals. Example: "Raising money to fly to the Georgia Comedy Film Festival. $400 plane tickets, $100 airport transportation, $100 for meals, staying with my cousin in midtown. I just need a little boost. I'll make sure to take pics and send updates on Instagram." Make it a cool experience and let people know your limitations. "I'm using 12 hours of PTO from my job. My Mom is dropping me off at the airport, I just need a little help. I can't believe we're nominated for an award! Even $25 helps. Thank you in advance."

If you can't make it, use your social media accounts to buy someone a ticket that lives locally and represents you. "I can't make it from the UK to Austin next month for this event, I am booked on a job. Can anyone in Texas make the trip? I'll pay for two event tickets and shirts. I wish I could be there. The event looks fun! Message me on Facebook."

Ask the festival if they can defer your screening. We deal with this all the time. "Hey Mikel, thanks for the acceptance to the Texas Short Film Festival. My buddy is getting married on that exact day in March and I can't make it. I see that you have multiple events per year, can we screen in your October screening, I'd really like to be there." This gives you time to plan further ahead. Cheaper airfare and more time to work your side hustle, build up PTO or find a replacement to attend on your behalf. Some festivals have multiple events per year, others do not. It doesn't hurt to ask.

At times, the financial demands of attending a film festival might stretch beyond your reach. When faced with such a scenario, there's no need to fret. A simple, heartfelt email to the festival organizers expressing your gratitude for the acceptance can go a long way. Let them know you'll be keeping up with the event via social media.

Your online presence can still make a significant impact. Engaging with posts, offering words of encouragement to fellow filmmakers and screenwriters with a supportive 'like' or 'comment', fosters a sense of community and solidarity. Consider supporting the festival in smaller, yet meaningful ways, like purchasing a festival-themed shirt or coffee mug. These gestures, though small, contribute to the festival's atmosphere and demonstrate your support without straining your finances. Remember, our presence isn't limited to physical locations; we can still be part of the festival spirit from afar, doing what we can without overextending ourselves financially.

Chapter 16: The Truth About Film Festival Waivers

Navigating the world of film festival submissions can be challenging, especially when it comes to managing budgets and submission fees. At FilmFestivalCircuit.com, where we manage over 10 different festivals, we receive a high volume of full fee waiver requests daily. We choose not to issue these waivers to maintain fairness for filmmakers and screenwriters who have paid their submission fees. If your strategy involves frequently requesting waivers, it's important to be cautious to avoid being labeled as a spammer, which could jeopardize your future email communications.

When seeking financial assistance, consider asking for partial waivers or discounts, demonstrating your willingness to invest in the process. Personalized emails are key. Here's an example of an effective email we received, with the name changed for privacy:

> *Hi, my name is Zach Barker. I directed a 7-minute short documentary film and am interested in submitting it to the Oregon Documentary Film Festival. Your festival's history of screening documentaries in theaters and drive-ins is impressive. We would love to see our film on the big screen in Oregon and are excited about the possibility of attending if selected. Are there any promo codes or discounts available for submissions right now? Any assistance would be greatly appreciated as we try to maximize our festival submissions budget. Thank you.*

If you're in a position where full fee waivers are your only option, remember these tips for requesting 100% waivers without being flagged as a spammer:

- Address Specific Individuals: Avoid generic salutations like "To Whom It May Concern." Try to address a specific person at the festival.
- Explain Your Interest: Clearly articulate why you're interested in that particular festival. For instance, "I'm drawn to the Philadelphia SciFi Film Festival because it's a key event for filmmakers in my genre and close to my location."
- Offer Marketing Support: Mention how you can help promote the festival, such as sharing content with your social media followers.
- Discuss Attendance Possibilities: Indicate whether you or someone from your team can attend the event, adding a personal touch to your submission.
- Propose a Press Release: Offer to contact local media for interviews and publicity about your film's screening, if selected.

The relationship between filmmakers and film festivals is fundamentally collaborative. Boasting about past festival achievements or displaying a sense of entitlement is less effective than showing a willingness to work together and adding value. We get emails like this multiple times per day:

> *Dear Programming Department, I wanted to kindly ask you if there is a possibility of a waiver fee for a low budget documentary feature from Nova Scotia. Our film festival budget is exhausted after getting accepted and winning awards at 25 film festivals so far. In Greece, Romania, New York, California, Ireland, Italy, UAE, Austria, Arizona, Zagreb and much more. This film is about maintaining family relationships and love. Please help us, we cannot afford any more submission fees.*

Let me translate this email for you.

> *This is a generic email. If I play the numbers game and spam enough film festivals, we will get into more film festivals and get more awards without spending the money that other submitters are spending, because they haven't mastered the art of mail merging like we have. We spent our money on 25 film festivals that we prioritized over yours and because we are awesome, you should give us a full fee waiver. We'll even include the name of your film festival in our next spam email, so that we can use your reputation to help get more fee waivers. We offer nothing. No social media engagement, press releases, attendance or anything of value. If you email us back, it's likely to go to our spam folder because we've used and abused this email address so much, communication will be next to impossible.*

Personalized communication, rather than generic emails, is more respectful and likely to be successful. In the current climate, particularly in economic conditions in 2024, filmmakers, screenwriters, and film festivals often operate with limited budgets. Therefore, empathy and cooperation are essential. Filmmaking involves not just creativity but also financial management. Balancing your budget and making informed choices is crucial to sustain your film festival aspirations without overspending.

Ideally, submission fees and event tickets wouldn't be necessary. We'd love to afford luxuries like limousines, large venues, airline tickets, hotels, and paparazzi, but the truth is that 99% of film festivals and filmmakers operate within a realistic budget, far from the extravagant Hollywood fantasy. It's important to plan ahead, exercise patience, and prepare a budget that covers the costs of submitting to events on the film festival circuit.

Chapter 17: I Got Into A Film Festival! Now what?

Congratulations on getting accepted into a film festival! This is indeed a significant milestone in your filmmaking journey. Here's a detailed plan to navigate through this exciting phase:

Understanding What a Film Festival Is:
- A film festival is a platform where creative works like films and screenplays are showcased, evaluated, and celebrated. It's a competitive event where your work is recognized by a jury and audience, offering valuable exposure and networking opportunities. Your acceptance into a festival is a testament to the quality of your work and should be a source of pride.

Expressing Gratitude to the Film Festival:
- Definitely, send a thank you email to the festival organizers. This shows professionalism and gratitude for the opportunity and recognition they've provided. Mention how the selection is meaningful for your career, and express enthusiasm for participating in the festival.

Announcing Your Achievement:
- Share your excitement and achievement on social media platforms. Post the laurels or certificate you received, mention the film festival, and provide a link to the festival's webpage where tickets or additional information are available. This not only celebrates your success but also promotes the festival.

Coordinating with Your Team:
- Contact your team members and contributors to check their availability for attending the festival. Inform the festival organizers about your and your team's attendance plans so they can prepare any necessary arrangements or acknowledgments.

Attending the Festival:
- If attending, focus on networking and learning opportunities. Engage with other filmmakers, attend different screenings, and participate in discussions. Festivals are not just about showcasing your work, but also about building relationships and gaining insights into the industry.

Supporting the Event Remotely If You Can't Attend:
- Offer to participate in remote interviews or podcasts.
- Promote the festival on your social media platforms.
- Engage with the festival and other participants online.
- Consider sending out a press release to highlight your film's selection and any nominations.

Keeping Everyone Updated:
- Regular updates on social media are effective. For those not active online, periodic emails or messages can keep them in the loop. Encourage your network to engage with your social media content.

Post-Festival Recap:
- After the event, thank the festival organizers again for the opportunity. Follow up with any contacts you made, either in person or virtually. This helps extend the networking benefits beyond the event.

Updating Marketing Materials
- Now that your work has been recognized, update your marketing materials. Add award laurels to your film's poster and share these updates on social media and other platforms. Also, refresh your personal media kit or headshot with images from the festival.

Remember, a film festival is not just about the recognition but also about the experience, learning, and connections you make. Enjoy this journey, and best of luck with your future endeavors in filmmaking!

Chapter 18: How To Send Out A Free Press Release

There are several websites where you can submit press releases. Each site varies in terms of features and reach and they offer free trials and free press releases on a limited basis. Here are some of the top recommended sites for 2024:

1. https://www.prlog.org/ - Known for its massive audience and high domain authority, PRLog offers basic submissions for free with decent visibility and distribution.
2. https://www.pr.com/ - PR.com is a comprehensive platform that offers free press release distribution along with business directory listings.
3. https://www.openpr.com/ - OpenPR provides free press release distribution services globally.
4. https://pressbox.com/ - Pressbox offers free press release submission services and distribution to media outlets and journalists.
5. https://prmediaonline.com/ - This site offers both free and premium press release distribution services.
6. https://www.prfire.com/ - PRFire allows for free press release submissions with options for multimedia elements.
7. https://www.1888pressrelease.com/ - This platform provides free press release submission with additional premium services available.
8. https://www.pr-inside.com/ - A simple platform that includes international news.
9. https://www.marketpressrelease.com/ - This site limits free submissions to one press release per day.
10. http://prsync.com/ - Requires creating a free account before submission.
11. https://www.freeprnow.com/ - Every press release appears on the homepage and shows a count of views.
12. https://www.enewswire.co.uk/ - A UK-based news site with a user-friendly form for submissions.
13. https://www.prfree.org/ - Offers distribution to search engines.
14. https://www.travpr.com/ - Focuses on travel-related press releases including film festivals.

These sites offer various benefits, including link building, increased online visibility, reduced marketing costs, and long-term online presence. However, it's important to remember that free press release sites may have limitations in reach, credibility, and features compared to paid services. If you find a PR site that is effective, it's worth the money to subscribe or pay for press release services that offer to boost your reach. Try them out first.

Chapter 19: Final Thoughts On the Film Festival Submissions Process

As we close this journey together, I sincerely hope the insights shared in these pages have illuminated your path in the dynamic world of film festivals. The realm we navigate is indeed competitive, yet brimming with opportunity. As a dedicated filmmaker or screenwriter, fortifying your submission is key to standing out. Let my experiences, both the missteps and the triumphs, be your guide. And remember, the wisdom gleaned from the common errors I've witnessed can be your secret weapon in this cinematic quest.

Imagine this book as a catalyst, boosting your acceptance rate into more festivals by even 20%. Such a leap not only signifies immense savings but is a testament to the value this guide brings, repaying your investment manifold. The strategies discussed here are rooted in practical, common-sense adjustments, attainable without heavy financial burdens. A modest investment of time and effort can yield remarkable results.

I eagerly anticipate the opportunity to witness your creative expressions and share a moment of connection at future film festivals. Your queries and suggestions for upcoming editions are invaluable; feel free to reach out to me at mikel.fair@filmfestivalcircuit.com. Your support through this purchase plays a crucial role in sustaining our dedicated staff and judges nationwide, ensuring the continued vibrancy of these events.

Looking ahead to 2024, I am filled with excitement at the prospect of meeting many of you at our festivals. Consider sharing the gift of knowledge by passing this book onto a friend immersed in the film industry, who might soon navigate the intricacies of film festival marketing. Wishing you all the best in your cinematic endeavors. Here's to your success and the thrilling journey ahead! If you have any suggestions for the next edition of this book, please contact me.

Film Festival Director Mikel Fair
https://www.filmfestivalcircuit.com

Chapter 20: Bonus Article: How Do I Get Accepted To Film Festivals in 2024?

This is a copy of the most popular article on my blog. I've updated it and included it in this book. My name is Mikel Fair and I've been a film festival director for over 15 years. This article offers 10 tips to help filmmakers and screenwriters get their films, screenplays, music videos, and series episodes into film festivals in 2024. A lot has changed in the industry since 2008 when my company, Film Festival Circuit, started accepting submissions for the first **Houston Comedy Film Festival (Link)** in Texas. This article provides insights into the competitive nature of film festivals, the importance of knowing your audience, and tips for successful submissions. The film festival submissions process can be highly competitive, with hundreds of submissions vying for a spot. To even be on par with other highly rated films and screenplays, your submission, at a minimum, needs to be strong in these ten areas.If you'd like to get more valuable insights about the Film Festival Submissions process, please get a copy of my ebook, The **Film Festival Submitters Handbook 2024 (Link) edition**. This 50 page book will dig deeper into this topic and help you create a successful plan for conquering the Film Festival Circuit in 2024. Avoid common costly mistakes that other filmmakers and screenwriters are making every day. I promise you, this will be the smartest $9.99 you've ever spent.

Tip #1: Total Runtime Is Critical For Film Scheduling

For films, ensure that you have the tightest edit with good pacing available. The number one negative determining factor, in my film festival director experience, is boredom. Your film must be dynamic, and every scene should contribute to your presentation. Getting bogged down in beautiful cinematography for lengthy periods, or having long-winded conversations that don't advance the storyline, is considered wasteful. If the judges, who are not familiar with your work, think that your film is slow, imagine what the audience will think. You don't want your film screening to turn into a bathroom break for half of the audience. You may think, "Our crew put a lot of hours into this" or "We spent a lot of money on this location." The last thing you want is to feel that you're discarding valuable parts of your film. I'm not recommending a hatchet job, where you remove entire scenes to meet an artificial time limit like 10 or 20 minutes. However, gaps in conversation, long transitions, and extended shots of someone thinking driving can become tedious. Some filmmakers have said to me, "I don't know what to cut because I'm too close to it." This can be a challenging situation and you may need a fresh set of eyes. Years ago, I used to invite guests to my house to watch the short films I produced. I'd create a fun atmosphere, not revealing too much of the story, and have plenty of cold drinks, popcorn, and movie candy. Then we'd sit down to watch a film. Having seen the film 100 times, I wouldn't need to watch it; instead, I'd keep an eye on my audience. Taking notes about their reactions with timestamps will start to reveal aspects of your edit that need tightening up, depending on your film's genre. Are they yawning, checking their phones, laughing, crying, getting tense? Their reactions gave me insight on where I could tighten up the edit.

Tip #2: Screenplay Length Matters

Similarly, long screenplays can be problematic. When I open a screenplay file for the first time and it's 135 pages, I think, "This is going to take a while." To be clear, if you're writing a screenplay, your intention is to create a roadmap for a production team to create a visual product based on your words. A screenplay isn't a novel and shouldn't be written as one. Roughly, 135 pages translate into 135 minutes of runtime. This can vary depending on the editor and other factors, but it's a general estimate. How many 135-minute feature films have you seen lately? Unless it's strategically an epic film like 'Lord of the Rings' or 'Napoleon', I can understand why your writing is this lengthy. However, for a comedy or horror film, this length probably means a lot of long-winded filler. I recommend keeping your feature-length screenplays under 120 pages, regardless of genre. If you're writing a short, it should be short. Is a 42-page screenplay really a short film? And if you're writing a long screenplay for some reason, your writer's statement should explain why. Start your film or screenplay strongly to captivate festival curators and viewers right from the start. The first scene should be impressive. Some of the best film screenings I've ever seen usually start with a scene that grabs everyone's attention, whether it's funny, action-packed, or features a cool montage edit. Hook the reader and make them stay until the end.

Tip #3: Online Release vs. Festival Recognition

Consider whether you want to reach a wide audience quickly by putting your film online for free public viewing or if you prefer recognition and critical acclaim through festivals. This is a common dilemma I see, especially with new filmmakers. They are so excited to complete their film that they share it with the world on YouTube or Vimeo and try to get a lot of views. For short or feature films that are meant for festivals, this may not be a great strategy. If any potential attendee searches for your film to find more information, they might find the entire film online, which may mean that they skip your film screening session at a film festival because they can always watch it at home. It's important to present your screening as a special experience. It's hard to create FOMO (fear of missing out) when your film is already available online. Conversely, if you are presenting a series online with multiple episodes, getting views and accolades can work in your favor. Getting traction for an entire series can be challenging, but a successful film festival run can attract new viewers at every festival. If you have a series, screening the pilot at the festival and not the entire series might be sufficient. There are some festivals that accept entire series with multiple episodes and screen them. At filmfestivalcirciut.com, every series episode must stand on its own. Accepting one episode does not mean that we are accepting all of them. Especially ones that we've never seen. We have a micro category for episodes that are six minutes or less and a regular series episode category for episodes that are 30 minutes or less. At the end of the credits of the episode you are submitting, you can include a QR code, a link to a website or social media page where viewers can continue watching more episodes.

As a screenwriter, I wouldn't make my screenplay publicly available without tracking who is downloading it. Even if I've registered this work with the **U.S. Copyright Office (Link)** and the **WGA West Registry (Link)** for protection. On your website, you should create a form that allows film industry professionals or members of the media to request your screenplay for review. Use this form as a lead generator, so that you can follow up with the person that requested it. Our film festivals do not send screenplays to anyone outside of our organization. If we receive a request for a screenplay, we forward the email to the screenwriter.

Tip #4: Research Festivals That Align With Your Niche

Most filmmakers and screenwriters spend their entire film festival submission budget on the largest historic festivals and Academy Award-qualifying festivals. It's commonly treated like a lottery. The common thought process is if your submission is accepted to one of the "big ones," then agents, distributors, investors, and producers with large checks are going to kick down your door and pay you for your work. If that doesn't work out initially, it's time to get serious about researching specific festivals that may fit your genre. For example, the **Oregon Screams Horror Film Festival (Link)** is pretty self-explanatory. If you have a film or screenplay in the horror or horror comedy genre, submitting to this event is a no-brainer. The **Oregon Documentary Film Festival (Link)** has been screening documentaries for almost 10 years now. The audience expects to experience this genre specifically. When the audience walks into the **Austin Comedy Film Festival (Link)** they expect the focus to be on films and stories that are created to generate laughter.

Over my 15 years of experience, I've observed that film festivals accepting all categories and genres, such as the **Texas Short Film Festival in San Antonio (Link)**, **Oregon Short Film Festival (Link)**, **Austin Short Film Festival (Link)**, and **Atlanta Short Film Festival (Link)**, attract the largest audiences and receive the most submissions. This is because they welcome a broad range of filmmakers and screenwriters, showcasing diverse content like music videos, action TV pilots, mockumentary films, student films, family dramas, science fiction screenplays, and environmental documentaries, appealing to a varied audience. These festivals do have a specialty that is important to consider. They do not screen feature films, which means that there's more available screen time to accept and schedule more film screenings.

Conversely, festivals targeting mature content, like the **Austin After Dark Film Festival (Link)** or the **Atlanta After Dark Film Festival (Link)**, often receive only half the submissions compared to all-genre festivals. However, this translates to less competition for submissions such as Dark Fantasy, Horror, or Dark Comedy Animation, which may be less common at more mainstream festivals due to their audience preferences.

Looking ahead to 2024, the aim for filmmakers and screenwriters should be to build a portfolio by getting accepted into as many festivals as possible. Gaining recognition and awards is a key strategy for gaining momentum in the industry. While investing heavily in the "big festivals" might seem appealing, it can be risky, as your work may be just one among thousands of submissions they review. In contrast, specialty festivals often provide a more welcoming platform, giving each submission thorough consideration from start to finish.

Tip #5: Be Prepared To Invest In Submission Fees

Submission fees are necessary for a successful festival to operate year over year. Consider these costs as part of your film's budget. Use platforms like **https://filmfestivalcircuit.com/** to simplify the submission process and find suitable festivals. If you visit right now, you can see the entire slate of film festivals planned in our network for 2024. Each festival has a different group of judges, and the results may vary depending on the city to which you're submitting. Additionally, you can request to review all five of the **judging scorecards (Link)** as a premium option for $25 once the judge's reviews are completed. This information is vital and can give you an edge in your submission journey. If you read several comments about your screenplay being too long or having too much profanity, you have the option to make adjustments before the final deadline. Or, if your film has low audio in a few scenes, you have time to correct these errors before the final deadline. Also, at **https://filmfestivalcircuit.com/** we have a single submission form that you can use for multiple events. The more festivals you submit to, the more you get for free. Check it out when you get a chance.

Tip #6: Create a Compelling Trailer

A well-crafted trailer for your film can capture the attention of festival organizers, as well as potential agents, distributors, investors, producers, and casual viewers. Think about this: If someone in the film industry were to research your film by searching for the director's name or the film's title on search engines, what information would they come across?Ideally, when they search, they will find a YouTube trailer of your film that has significant engagement, such as numerous likes, shares, and comments. High engagement on social media can help generate interest and establish a track record for your work.I have observed that several filmmakers opt to upload their trailers on Vimeo, possibly due to its superior video quality. However, Vimeo is not as high-engagement of a platform compared to YouTube. Moreover, Google and YouTube are closely connected from a business perspective, which may result in better search results on YouTube. Creating a trailer doesn't have to be complex. Simply include some high-resolution screenshots, short video clips, behind-the-scenes photos, and essential credits like "directed by" or "starring..." At the end of the trailer, include a call to action such as "follow us for updates" or "subscribe for updates" along with a social media link. Avoid mentioning specific screening dates, like "coming October 26th, 2023," to prevent the trailer from appearing outdated after that date has passed.

Tip #7: Avoid Submitting Rough Cuts And Early Drafts

Make sure your film or screenplay is in its best possible condition before submitting, as each festival judge usually reviews it once. Steer clear of rough cuts, rough drafts, and works-in-progress, as your film or screenplay will be evaluated alongside completed and polished works. You don't want your film or screenplay to come across as incomplete, rough, or amateurish. If you're eager to submit your screenplay or film before a particular deadline, utilize your writer's or director's statement to explain the motivation behind that submission and its current stage. You might need to color correct the video or add sound effects. As a screenwriter, you could be waiting for script coverage or feedback from scorecards at another festival. Be as open about this as possible. In our festivals, if selected, you have the option to defer until the next season if you can't complete your edit before the file delivery deadline.

Tip #8: Properly Package Your Submission

Supporting materials, like posters, trailers, synopses, and director's and writer's statements, along with social media links, should be professionally executed and engaging to enhance your submission. There are various sections on the film festival submission form that you can complete to convey your film's story and create its virtual package. Are you filling out your submission forms as thoroughly as your competitors? Upon examining our group of submissions for the Austin Comedy Film Festival in the fall of 2023, I discovered that half of the submitters provided a synopsis for their film or screenplay that was only one sentence long or they provided nothing at all. A synopsis should be at least 3-5 sentences in length. How can you describe your film to someone in just one sentence? That may work for a tagline, but not for a synopsis. In the same film festival, half of the submitters didn't include a poster with the director's name on it. When was the last time you walked into a movie theater and saw a poster for a film without credits on it? Every film poster for any major theatrical release has an informative poster. If someone researches your film or screenplay online, your poster should be the first image they see, representing your film or screenplay. If your film has the same title as another, how does someone know if your short film called "Blind Date" is the correct one they saw at the film festival last week? A lack of information can lead to a lack of interest. Don't be one of those submitters who leaves half of their submission form blank. You only get one chance to make a first impression.

Tip #9: Pump It Up On Social Media

In 2024, it's widely accepted that social media is an integral part of our society and not just a passing trend. This is also an important factor in getting selected for film festivals, as a strong social media presence can help build your following, which is highly valued by film festivals, distributors, agents, producers, and investors.

As mentioned earlier, when someone uses a search engine to research your name, what will they find? If someone wants to research you, which link are you providing them? If you're active on X (Twitter), consider creating a verified account dedicated to your screenwriting, acting, or directing endeavors. Here are some suggestions on what to post about:

- Share updates on your latest projects, such as scriptwriting, acting roles, or directing experiences.
- Post behind-the-scenes photos and videos from your film sets or rehearsals.
- Share interesting articles, news, or trends related to your field.
- Engage with your audience by asking questions or hosting polls related to your work.
- Offer insights and advice to aspiring screenwriters, actors, or directors.

Remember, social media is a powerful tool for promoting your work and connecting with your audience. Use it wisely and consistently to make the most of its potential. Here are a few sentences to help you write great posts:

1. *I just got accepted to a film festival, I'm feeling great.*
2. *My screenplay or film was just nominated for an award at this film festival.*
3. *If you'd like to check out my film screening, save the date for this film festival.*
4. *The awards program for this film festival is on this date. Wish me luck.*
5. *I just updated my poster with a new laurel from this film festival, check it out.*
6. *I haven't seen my college roommate in 8 years; we met at this film festival. Check out the photo.*
7. *I met an amazing actress at this film festival. Her film is so cool; here's a link to the trailer.*
8. *After watching my film on screen, I think I'm going to change the edit just slightly.*
9. *I read a short romantic comedy screenplay from this amazing writer I met at this film festival. I'm gathering a crew to produce it.*
10. *I got accepted to two film festivals on the same weekend. Should I go to Florida or Arizona? Any thoughts?*

Active engagement is exciting. On almost every social media platform, you can plan your posts and schedule their release. So, you can spend an hour or two on Sunday, scheduling two or three posts to be released during the week during business hours, so that your profile remains active. Think about your creative work as a snowball. You want to keep building momentum throughout the year. Being active isn't just posting. You can also like, share, and comment on other posts as well. When you are actively supporting others, they are more likely to support you as well with engagement.

Tip #10: Email the Film Festival Before You Submit

This is a simple strategy that can reveal a lot about where you are submitting. If a film festival doesn't respond to your email within three months, what will the communication be like? Are you receiving form letters in return, or is a bot answering you? If you don't ask a question, you may not get a response at all. If your email simply states, "Just letting you know that we submitted a film, thanks for your consideration," then don't expect a response. It's a good idea to send an email that includes at least one question.

Firstly, let the festival know that you're submitting to them for a specific reason. Avoid being generic. For example, say, "I'm letting you know that I plan to submit to your event because it's the only sci-fi film festival in the state of Virginia, and I want to make sure that my screenplay is read by film festival judges who like this genre."

Secondly, inform the film festival if you, a member of your crew, or a friend plans to attend. For instance, "If accepted, my uncle in Detroit will be attending the festival on my behalf with his wife. They have never been to a film festival before and would love to experience it all." This shows that you're bringing more value to the film festival than just a submission. Attendance is important for every event, and perhaps the festival will evaluate your film or screenplay sooner and accept it early. What if you can't make it? No problem, let the festival know that you plan to bring other value. For example, "If accepted, I would love to blast the news out on my X (Twitter) account. I have 23,000 followers and would love to give away some tickets for the event. I live in the UK, but I have plenty of supporters in the US who are interested in seeing my film live."

Thirdly, inquire about promo codes or discounts. If you can save 20% here or 25% there, it can really stretch your film festival submissions budget, and this compels the festival to respond to you. I can tell you firsthand that filmmakers request outright 100% fee waivers with generic emails 20 or 30 times per day. It's impossible for a festival to survive giving away hundreds of fee waivers unless the owners of the events are millionaires. Most full waiver requests end up in the recycle bin. I suggest asking for a discount, as this indicates a willingness on your part to contribute to the festival and respect the time and money that it takes to put on any event of any size. Film festivals want your business and should notify you of a sale or promo code fairly quickly. Don't expect the most famous festivals in the world to offer discounts. When you're getting 18,000 submissions and only accepting 100, most of those major film festivals aren't going to respond. If you get a human response from a film festival pretty quickly, then you can trust that the email address for the festival is closely monitored. If you have questions about the schedule, file delivery, or awards once you've been accepted, it's nice to know that you have a reliable open line of communication.

Article Conclusion

Since launching our first event in 2008, there have been significant changes. Social media has become more active, and businesses are increasingly using automated responses and bots for communication. The economy has seen notable fluctuations in recent years, impacting film festival submission budgets, which were reduced. Particularly in 2020 and 2021, film production significantly slowed down, leading to fewer submissions, partly due to extended strikes involving writers and actors. However, the landscape in 2024 is looking up. Film production is accelerating, the economy is showing signs of recovery, and the demand for quality content is at an all-time high. With a hundred streaming networks now actively seeking content, numerous festivals have weathered the economic challenges and are expanding their offerings more than ever before.

Now is an opportune moment for you to make your mark. I encourage you to submit your work to as many festivals as possible and strive to attend them to gain the complete film festival experience. The year 2024 could be pivotal for you. Best of luck.

Index A: Film Festival Circuit Film/Video Category List

This is a complete list of film and video submission categories for the events that we own and operate at https://filmfestivalcircuit.com/. Our company focuses on content that is 30 minutes or less including credits. The only exceptions being, that in 2024, we are accepting feature film submissions at the Oregon Screams Horror Film Festival and the Oregon Documentary Film Festival. We hope to add more film festivals that screen feature films in the coming years. Here is a list of categories that you can submit to. This list may differ from other festivals in the industry.

1. Action Film
2. Animated Film
3. Animated Comedy Film
4. Black History Documentary
5. Comedy Film
6. Comedy Series Episode
7. Dark Comedy Film
8. Dark Comedy Series Episode
9. Dark Drama Film
10. Dark Drama Series Episode
11. Dark Fantasy Film
12. Dark Science Fiction Film
13. Documentary Film
14. Documentary Series Episode
15. Drama Film
16. Drama Series Episode
17. Experimental Documentary Film
18. Experimental Film
19. Experimental Horror Film
20. Fantasy Film
21. Found Footage Comedy Film
22. Found Footage Horror Film
23. Horror Comedy Film
24. Horror Comedy Series Episode
25. Horror Film
26. Horror Series Episode
27. Mockumentary Film
28. Mockumentary Series Episode
29. Music Video
30. Music Video (Comedy)
31. Music Video (Documentary)
32. Music Video (Experimental)
33. Music Video (Horror)
34. Proof Of Concept
35. Relationship Drama Film
36. Relationship Drama Series Episode

37. Romantic Comedy Film
38. Romantic Comedy Series Episode
39. Science Fiction Film
40. Short Film
41. Sketch Comedy
42. Stand-Up Comedy
43. Suspense Thriller Film

Index B: Film Festival Circuit Screenplay/Teleplay Category List

This is a complete list of screenplay and teleplay submissions categories for the events managed by https://filmfestivalcircuit.com/ Each city and event has their own set of judges that reads each screenplay from beginning to end before leaving a rating. The judges are not required to issue every single award listed. This is the list that they can choose from.

1. Comedy Feature Screenplay
2. Comedy Series Episode (Teleplay)
3. Comedy Short Screenplay
4. Dark Comedy Feature Screenplay
5. Dark Comedy Series Episode (Teleplay)
6. Dark Comedy Short Screenplay
7. Dark Drama Feature Screenplay
8. Dark Drama Series Episode (Teleplay)
9. Dark Drama Short Screenplay
10. Dark Fantasy Feature Screenplay
11. Dark Fantasy Short Screenplay
12. Dark Science Fiction Feature Screenplay
13. Dark Science Fiction Short Screenplay
14. Drama Feature Screenplay
15. Drama Series Episode (Teleplay)
16. Drama Short Screenplay
17. Fantasy Feature Screenplay
18. Fantasy Short Screenplay
19. Horror Comedy Feature Screenplay
20. Horror Comedy Series Episode (Teleplay)
21. Horror Comedy Short Screenplay
22. Horror Feature Screenplay
23. Horror Series Episode (Teleplay)
24. Horror Short Screenplay
25. Relationship Drama Feature Screenplay
26. Relationship Drama Series Episode (Teleplay)
27. Relationship Drama Short Screenplay
28. Romantic Comedy Feature Screenplay
29. Romantic Comedy Series Episode (Teleplay)
30. Romantic Comedy Short Screenplay
31. Science Fiction Feature Screenplay
32. Science Fiction Short Screenplay

Index C: Film Festival Circuit Film/Video Awards List

This is a list of film and video awards that our festivals give to the highest rated films in each submission category at https://filmfestivalcircuit.com/ The judges are not required to issue every single award listed. This is the list that they can choose from.

1. Best Action Film Award
2. Best Action Micro Film Award
3. Best Animated Comedy Film Award
4. Best Animated Film Award
5. Best Animated Micro Film Award
6. Best Black History Documentary Film Award
7. Best Comedy Film Award
8. Best Comedy Micro Film Award
9. Best Comedy Micro Series Episode Award
10. Best Comedy Series Episode Award
11. Best Dark Comedy Film Award
12. Best Dark Comedy Micro Film Award
13. Best Dark Comedy Series Episode Award
14. Best Dark Drama Film Award
15. Best Dark Drama Micro Film Award
16. Best Dark Drama Series Episode Award
17. Best Dark Fantasy Film Award
18. Best Dark Fantasy Micro Film Award
19. Best Dark Science Fiction Film Award
20. Best Dark Science Fiction Micro Film Award
21. Best Documentary Film Award
22. Best Documentary Micro Film Award
23. Best Documentary Music Video Award
24. Best Documentary Series Episode Award
25. Best Drama Film Award
26. Best Drama Micro Film Award
27. Best Drama Series Episode Award
28. Best Experimental Documentary Film Award
29. Best Experimental Film Award
30. Best Experimental Horror Film Award
31. Best Experimental Micro Film Award
32. Best Experimental Music Video Award
33. Best Fantasy Film Award
34. Best Fantasy Micro Film Award
35. Best Found Footage Comedy Film Award
36. Best Found Footage Horror Film Award

37. Best Horror Comedy Film Award
38. Best Horror Comedy Micro Film Award
39. Best Horror Comedy Series Episode Award
40. Best Horror Film Award
41. Best Horror Micro Film Award
42. Best Horror Music Video Award
43. Best Horror Series Episode Award
44. Best Mockumentary Film Award
45. Best Mockumentary Micro Film Award
46. Best Mockumentary Series Episode Award
47. Best Music Video Award
48. Best Relationship Drama Film Award
49. Best Relationship Drama Micro Film Award
50. Best Relationship Drama Series Episode Award
51. Best Romantic Comedy Film Award
52. Best Romantic Comedy Micro Film Award
53. Best Science Fiction Film Award
54. Best Science Fiction Micro Film Award
55. Best Sketch Comedy Film Award
56. Best Stand-Up Comedy Video Award
57. Best Suspense Thriller Film Award
58. Funniest Music Video Award

Index D: Film Festival Circuit Screenplay/Teleplay Awards List

This is a list of screenplay and teleplay awards that our festivals give to the highest rated films in each submission category at https://filmfestivalcircuit.com/ The judges are not required to issue every single award listed. This is the list that they can choose from.

1. Best Comedy Feature Screenplay Award
2. Best Comedy Short Screenplay Award
3. Best Comedy Teleplay Award
4. Best Dark Comedy Feature Screenplay Award
5. Best Dark Comedy Screenplay Award
6. Best Dark Comedy Short Screenplay Award
7. Best Dark Comedy Teleplay Award
8. Best Dark Drama Feature Screenplay Award
9. Best Dark Drama Short Screenplay Award
10. Best Dark Drama Teleplay Award
11. Best Dark Fantasy Screenplay Award
12. Best Dark Science Fiction Feature Screenplay Award
13. Best Dark Science Fiction Screenplay Award
14. Best Dark Science Fiction Short Screenplay Award
15. Best Drama Feature Screenplay Award
16. Best Drama Short Screenplay Award
17. Best Drama Teleplay Award
18. Best Fantasy Feature Screenplay Award
19. Best Fantasy Screenplay Award
20. Best Fantasy Short Screenplay Award
21. Best Horror Comedy Feature Screenplay Award
22. Best Horror Comedy Screenplay Award
23. Best Horror Comedy Short Screenplay Award
24. Best Horror Comedy Teleplay Award
25. Best Horror Feature Screenplay Award
26. Best Horror Short Screenplay Award
27. Best Horror Teleplay Award
28. Best Relationship Drama Feature Screenplay Award
29. Best Relationship Drama Screenplay Award
30. Best Relationship Drama Short Screenplay Award
31. Best Romantic Comedy Feature Screenplay Award
32. Best Romantic Comedy Screenplay Award
33. Best Romantic Comedy Short Screenplay Award
34. Best Romantic Comedy Teleplay Award
35. Best Science Fiction Feature Screenplay Award
36. Best Science Fiction Screenplay Award
37. Best Science Fiction Short Screenplay Award

Index E: Film Festival Circuit Non-Category Awards List

This is a list of awards that are not assigned to a specific category that all submissions are eligible for at https://filmfestivalcircuit.com/ The judges are not required to issue every single award listed. This is the list that they can choose from.

1. Best Acting Performance Award
2. Best Supporting Acting Performance Award
3. Best Cinematography Award
4. Best Director Award
5. Best Editing Award
6. Best Ensemble Cast Award
7. Best Georgia Feature Screenplay Award
8. Best Georgia Film Award
9. Best Georgia Micro Film Award
10. Best Georgia Short Screenplay Award
11. Best International Director Award
12. Best International Feature Screenplay Award
13. Best International Film Award
14. Best International Micro Film Award
15. Best International Short Screenplay Award
16. Best Oregon Feature Screenplay Award
17. Best Oregon Film Award
18. Best Oregon Micro Film Award
19. Best Oregon Short Screenplay Award
20. Best Original Music Award
21. Best Proof of Concept Award
22. Most Inspirational Film Award
23. Best Student Screenplay Award
24. Best Student Film Award
25. Best Texas Film Award
26. Best Texas Micro Film Award
27. Best Texas Screenplay Award
28. Best Texas Short Screenplay Award
29. Most Original Concept Award
30. Single Funniest Moment Award
31. Best Feature Length Screenplay Award
32. Best Screenplay Award
33. Best Short Screenplay
34. Best Trailer Award
35. Best Series Episode Award
36. Best Feature Film Award
37. Best Micro Film Award
38. Best Picture Award Award

www.ingramcontent.com/pod-product-compliance
Lightning Source LLC
Chambersburg PA
CBHW081205290526
45796CB00010B/342